LET LOVE RULE

LENNY KRAVITZ

with **DAVID RITZ**

LET LOVE RULE

sphere

SPHERE

First published in the United States by Henry Holt and Company
First published in Great Britain in 2020 by Sphere
This paperback edition published by Sphere in 2021

1 3 5 7 9 10 8 6 4 2

A CIP catalogue record for this book
is available from the British Library.

ISBN 978-0-7515-8210-9

Printed and bound in Great Britain by Clays Ltd, Elcograf S.p.A.

Papers used by Sphere are from well-managed forests
and other responsible sources.

Sphere
An imprint of
Little, Brown Book Group
Carmelite House
50 Victoria Embankment
London EC4Y 0DZ

An Hachette UK Company
www.hachette.co.uk

www.littlebrown.co.uk

For my mother

LET LOVE RULE

can't breathe.

Beneath the ground, the wooden casket I am trapped in is being lowered deeper and deeper into the cold, dark earth. Fear overtakes me as I fall into a paralytic state. I can hear the dirt being shoveled over me. My heart pounds through my chest. I can't scream, and if I could, who would hear me? Just as the final shovel of soil is being packed tightly over me, I convulse out of my nightmare into the sweat- and urine-soaked bed in the small apartment on the island of Manhattan that my family calls home. Shaken and disoriented, I make my way out of the tiny back bedroom into the pitch-dark living room, where my mother and father sleep on a convertible couch. I stand at the foot of their bed just staring . . . waiting.

What kind of dream is this for a five-year-old? What have I experienced to produce this kind of imagery? It's 1969. The only violence I've seen is in cartoons of Bugs Bunny and the Road Runner on the eight-inch black-and-white screen of our Singer portable television.

Mom senses my presence and awakens. What's wrong? I confess I've had a bad dream. She picks me up and carries me back to my bedroom. She quickly changes the sheets, brings a warm washcloth to wipe me down, and dresses me in fresh pajamas. She consoles me. I drift back to sleep.

This dream recurs countless times. Years pass before I understand its true meaning.

I now know that God was speaking to me. I believe the dream was telling me that life does not end in the grave. There's something beyond. Something eternal. But I don't want to get ahead of myself. I want to go back to the beginning of the journey.

MANHATTAN
AND BROOKLYN

GREENWICH VILLAGE, 1963

On the small bandstand of a cellar jazz club, where the air is thick with smoke and the lights are low, John Coltrane commands his rhythm section. With a gentle nod of his head, he sets an achingly slow groove. Elvin Jones effortlessly works his whisper-quiet brushes. McCoy Tyner plays a subtle piano intro. Bassist Jimmy Garrison provides a gentle heartbeat. Then Coltrane, breathing deeply, exhales into his horn. The sound of his tenor sax is startling—rich, lush, sultry.

At a corner table, a self-assured Jewish man looks into the eyes of a beguiling Afro-Caribbean woman.

She's my mother, Roxie Roker, and he's my dad, Sy Kravitz.

Dad's a thirty-nine-year-old journalist-producer for NBC News at 30 Rockefeller Center, in the heart of Midtown Manhattan. Years before, he started out as a page in this same building before working his way up. He's a self-starter. A former Army Green Beret who saw action in the Korean War, he's also a member of the Reserve. His parents, Joe and Jean Kravitz, live in Sheepshead Bay, Brooklyn, with many other Jews of Russian descent.

Dad's divorced with two daughters. He lives alone in a $350-a-month one-bedroom apartment at 5 East Eighty-Second Street, just off Central Park on the Upper East Side. A graduate of New York University, he's a sharp dresser and a consummate charmer. He loves music, especially jazz, and theater. He has his artistic side, but it's overpowered by order and discipline.

It's at 30 Rock where he meets Roxie Roker, age thirty-four. My mom is a soulful, deeply elegant person. An Alpha Kappa Alpha sorority member and drama major, she graduated from Howard University with honors before studying at the Shakespeare Institute at Stratford-upon-Avon, England, and joining a theater company in Copenhagen. She performs in Off-Broadway productions and supports herself working as an assistant to a high-ranking NBC boss. She's the ultimate executive secretary: efficient and graceful in every manner.

She has inherited the work ethic of her parents. Her Bahamian father, a self-made man, and her Georgia-born mother, who works as a domestic, own the home where she was raised in Bedford-Stuyvesant, Brooklyn.

Roxie has never dated a white man before. But it's not my father's skin color that bothers her. It's the fact that they work in the same office. She's also a little uneasy knowing he's been married and divorced. And the fact that he doesn't seem very close to his daughters. She is skeptical of his nature.

Dad takes Mom to a Broadway revival of *The Crucible*; they catch Thelonious Monk at the Five Spot; they see Alvin Ailey at City Center; they hear Langston Hughes read at the 92nd Street Y. Sy and Roxie are kindred spirits. He's determined to win her affection.

You see, now that he's found the most beguiling woman in New York City, Sy is confident. Roxie is intrigued and flattered by all the attention. She's delighted to have someone trek downtown to see her act in avant-garde plays. She's taken by his enthusiasm and perseverance, qualities that her own father taught her to appreciate.

Mom has dreams and ambitions. She is a bright young star: a talented, trained actress and a person of passion and poise. She suggests and later insists that Sy reach out to his two daughters and reconnect with them. For her, it's a deal breaker. He agrees, and despite his trepidation, a bond is forged.

In an alchemical way, Sy's and Roxie's dreams meld. They fall head over heels. He proposes. The next night, my mom goes to the Café Carlyle, on Madison Avenue, to consult with her dear buddy Bobby Short, the iconic cabaret singer and pianist. What does he think about her marrying Sy?

In his grand manner, Short responds, "Well, I don't see anyone else asking."

The wedding is a humble affair that Dad's parents, heartbroken that their son is marrying a Black woman (and a gentile to boot), refuse to attend. It takes my birth to bring them around. I love knowing that without doing a thing except existing, I bring peace to my family.

GEMINI

I am deeply two-sided: Black and white, Jewish and Christian, Manhattanite and Brooklynite.

My young life was all about opposites and extremes. As a kid, you take everything in stride. So, I accepted my Gemini soul. I owned it. In fact, I adored it. Yins and yangs mingled in various parts of my heart and mind, giving my life balance and fueling my curiosity, giving me comfort.

Though nightmares haunted me throughout childhood, once I was awake, I was ready to go. Awake and alive. Looking to explore. Looking for adventure. Many people remember their early years filled with trauma. Despite the drama and dysfunction I will regale you with, my story is not one born of darkness. My youth was filled with joy, and I was surrounded by what felt like endless, unconditional love. From my mother, from a dozen glamorous godmothers, from grandparents, from neighbors who felt like aunts and uncles, from sisters and cousins and friends who became my chosen family.

My father cared for me deeply as well, but it took me a while to realize it. He didn't know how to show me affection, and our relationship was strained because we were just so different. He lived in a framework of extreme discipline. I ran free. I was born messy and feral, like most little kids. Dad hated clutter and would scold me at the sight of a single toy left on the floor.

The thing is, the discipline never took. He was stubborn, and so was I. That quality we shared. I had a kind of rambunctious will that couldn't be locked down. He had the kind of authority that couldn't be challenged. Dad and I worked toward deeply disparate goals with equal fervor. Our differences would only deepen as time went on. It is only in recent years that I have begun to understand our incredible similarities. I am so grateful for his place in my life. He never ran out on me. He was there at critical times, offering me critical help. Our impasses were epic, but, as a result, I grew stronger. I simply would not be who I am today without those power struggles. As ugly as our battles became, they were an education. I had to go through Dad to become me.

Mom was and is my heart. It was Mom who hung the poster over my bed that read, "War Is Not Healthy for Children and Other Living Things." It was also Mom who painted the peace sign on my cheek and proudly walked me through antiwar marches in Central Park. Naturally, I didn't get the political implications, but I loved the excitement of the crowd singing "Give Peace a Chance." I felt like I was in the midst of an important moment. I felt protected by the goodness that radiated from Mom without her even having to try.

Her first form of protection was to make sure I knew who and where I was, in the most physical sense. To do that, she taught me my very first song. It had a sweet melody. I sang, "Leonard Albert Kravitz is my name. And I live at 5 East Eighty-Second Street in New York City. And I live at three-sixty-eight Throop Avenue with Grandma in Brooklyn."

Looking back, the song has more depth than I realized. In it lives the two-sided nature of my childhood. Twin worlds, twin identities. I was happy in both. Both formed me. I'm not sure how or why I could so easily slip in and out of starkly diverse cultures and yet remain confident in my own skin, but I could. I believe this intense adaptability gave me the freedom to be happy anywhere. Half a century later, I am still grateful.

Let me paint the picture for you.

In Manhattan, our apartment at 5 East Eighty-Second Street was on the third floor of a once-grand five-story home chopped up into a dozen modest units. In the sixties you could still find affordable housing on the now-exclusive Upper East Side. Our building, modeled on turn-of-the-century Parisian Beaux-Arts architecture, was a monument to faded glory: wrought iron decorated glass doors, carved cherubs, and an ornate lobby set off by a sweeping marble staircase with a tiny European elevator.

Set in the back of the building, our compact apartment looked out onto brick walls. No view. The living room had a small dining area and a spinet piano. There were shelves filled with jazz records and books like James Baldwin's *Go Tell It on the Mountain* and Sammy Davis Jr.'s *Yes I Can!*. Off to the side was a sliver of a galley kitchen. There was also a pullout couch where my parents slept. They gave me the only bedroom. That made me feel special. It also allowed Mom and Dad to give parties that wouldn't interfere with my sleep.

My parents had a huge network of fascinating friends whom they loved entertaining at our place. My room was filled with all the stuff little boys like: Hot Wheels, model planes, Frankenstein and the Wolfman figurines, and, best of all, a plastic record player.

Football legend Joe Namath lived across the street—sometimes he'd throw a ball around with us kids—and only a few steps away, at the end of our block, stood the mighty Metropolitan Museum of Art, like a fortress commanding the eastern border of Central Park.

Although our place was small, most of the kids in the neighborhood lived in enormous apartments. It was a world of privilege.

In contrast to all that, I didn't see much privilege in Brooklyn. Mom's parents lived across the East River in mostly Black Bedford-Stuyvesant. My early life was a dance between the two boroughs. I felt I belonged in both places—and the truth is, I did.

My education began at a nursery school in Brooklyn called Junior Academy. So, all week long, I'd stay with Mom's parents, who owned a three-story home at the corner of Throop Avenue and Kosciuszko Street, in the heart of Bed-Stuy. On Friday afternoons, my parents would pick me up in their VW Bug and drive me back to Manhattan for the weekend.

My life in Brooklyn was grounded by two phenomenal human beings, my maternal grandparents, Albert and Bessie Roker. They showered me, their only grandchild, with love. Born on the small, remote island of Inagua in the Bahamas, Grandpa was forced to become the man of the house at age nine, when his father died and left four children to the care of his ailing wife. Grandpa didn't have electricity or ice until his teens. Eventually he made his way to Miami, where Georgia-born southern belle Bessie was working in an ice-cream parlor. They fell in love, married, and migrated north to New York in search of a better life. The world has never seen a harder worker than Albert Roker. Doing four jobs at once, Grandpa was a house painter, doorman, handyman, and manual laborer at a factory where he wound up as foreman. He always spent less than he earned and managed his money with an eye toward his family's well-being and his daughter's education.

Grandpa used to talk about a vision that came to him as a kid: when he grew up, he'd never refuse anything his wife or child asked of him. The answer, he decided, would never be no. And it never was.

Albert loved learning. Completely self-educated, he knew the Bible; he quoted Shakespeare, Socrates, and Malcolm X. He devoured whole books in a single night. He was driven to improve his mind. He also did all he could to expose his daughter to important culture.

When my mother was thirteen, Grandpa took her to the theater to see *Porgy and Bess*, where they were forced to sit in the section "For Colored Only." Despite the irony—a musical featuring Black performers performed to an audience where Blacks were given second-class treatment—the production triggered my mother's interest in theater. Her father's prudent management of money put her through Howard University.

On Sunday mornings, Grandpa dressed me in a suit and tie, and off we went in his Cadillac to Lincoln Center, where, at Avery Fisher Hall, Dr. Ervin Seale presided at the nondenominational Church of the Truth. In his sermons, Dr. Seale praised the great teachers and prophets Buddha, Jesus, and Moses. Grandpa read all Dr. Seale's books, whose titles (*Ten Words That Will Change Your Life* and *Success Is You*) reflected his code of self-improvement as spiritual evolution. Though this compass was not exactly the same as mine would become, his sermons were an introduction to these concepts and an invitation to start forming my own connection to the unknown.

For all my father's powers and passions, devotion to God was not one. Grandpa was my guiding light for all that and more. He was also surrogate father to dozens of neighborhood boys. He took the kids bowling, drove them to the countryside to play golf, and got them tickets to museums and Broadway plays. He made sure they had library cards; he showed them how to apply to trade school and college. Grandpa saw life as an opportunity for self-improvement at every turn. The great thing about him, though, was that he didn't see it as an opportunity for just himself, but for everyone—especially kids who lacked resources. Grandpa became that resource for an entire neighborhood.

He was also a disciplinarian, but with a style much different from Dad's. If I was mischievous, Grandpa sat me down and, like a psychologist, explained how my bad behavior was hurting me more than anyone else. He droned on and on and on. He wanted me to understand *why* I'd done what I'd done, so that I could identify the problem and resolve it. The whole process was agonizing. I would have preferred a beating. But thank God he had insight and patience. His approach was invaluable.

Grandpa had a Bahamian Sidney Poitier–style accent; Grandma spoke with a slight Georgia drawl and attended a Methodist church. If he was intellect, she was soul. My grandmother was the love of my life. A full-bodied woman who loved her southern-fried cooking, Bessie possessed a God-given ability to read people right. When Grandpa went off on a philosophical rant, she'd look at him as if to say, "Albert, *please!*"

Back then, Bed-Stuy was a village, a community comprised of relocated people who, like Grandma, hailed from "Down South" or, like Grandpa, the Caribbean. It felt safe. When I think of Bed-Stuy, I think of Mother Sister, Ruby Dee's character in Spike Lee's *Do the Right Thing*, who watches over the neighborhood from her window. We had Mother Sisters everywhere. If my grandmother was at work and one of the Mother Sisters caught me doing wrong, she'd discipline me right then and there. Then she'd tell Grandma, which means I'd get my ass whupped a second time.

My grandmother was so protective of me and loved me so much that even if I got in trouble for a good reason, she would defend me. She'd deny I'd done it with every fiber of her being, and then, in private, she'd tear my behind up for what I'd done. Punishment was to teach, not to shame. So, she wasn't going to let anybody embarrass me. Still, her anger never lasted long. By evening, I'd be cuddled up in her bed, the two of us watching *I Love Lucy*, *The Honeymooners*, or her favorite, *The Lawrence Welk Show*.

Life with my grandparents in Bed-Stuy was not only its own distinct universe, but I was a whole other person there, with a whole other name. This came about because so many of our neighbors came from Down South. (*Down South* was the term everyone used. Until I learned otherwise, I thought Down South was the name of an actual city.) Most of the transplanted southerners retained their drawls. When I met Poppy Branch, the kid next door who had just moved from "Down South," his sister Renee asked me, "Whas yo naaaaaame?"

"Lennie."

"Eddie?"

"I said, Lennie."

"Oh, yeahhh. Eddie."

I gave up. And just like that, I became Eddie throughout Brooklyn. In Manhattan, I was Lennie (with an *ie*, as I used to spell it); and in Brooklyn, I was Eddie. My Gemini ass was pleased.

The streets excited me. This was a time—the late sixties and early seventies—when Bed-Stuy had not yet become a war zone. There was crime and scattered violence, but elders were still treated with respect. No matter what kind of deal was going down, if my grandfather walked by, he was greeted with, "Good afternoon, Mr. Roker." If my grandmother was walking home from the supermarket with an armful of groceries, the boys would insist on carrying them to her door.

I loved the characters strolling the sidewalks sporting their finest "tailor-mades," hand-sewn gabardine slacks by the man who ran the dry cleaner's. He was a big deal. He was hip. There were lots of platform shoes, gold chains, and blown-out Afros.

My buddies lived in apartments with paint peeling off the walls and cracked linoleum rolling up off the floor. We sat on milk crates and drank Kool-Aid out of jelly jars. Yet the places were full of life and love. No matter where I went, I was family. My friends' mothers treated me like their son. There was always an extra plate of chicken, red beans, and rice.

The soundtrack of Bed-Stuy was soul. Music was always in the air. James Brown endlessly spinning on someone's turntable. Certain songs stuck with me: Mrs. Maudie Osborne, who rented the third floor from my grandparents, loved to listen to Fontella Bass's "Rescue Me" while she drank her blues away. Not sure anyone ever did rescue her, but I sure did love the song.

The sights and sounds of Bed-Stuy: boomboxes, block parties, men crowded around tinny transistor radios blasting Mets and Yankee games, salsa music pulsating from an apartment building mainly populated by Puerto Ricans. Clothes hanging on lines across alleys. Girls jumping double dutch in front of bodegas where we bought miniature bottle rockets, put them on the ground, set them aflame, and, with giddy satisfaction, watched them take off after pedestrians—thus the nickname "nigger chasers." That was my bad boy mode.

In my good boy mode, I accompanied Grandma down DeKalb

Avenue to buy fresh whiting from the fish market. We'd stroll past the fruit and vegetable stand, the butchers and the barbers, the record store and the Chinese takeout with the bulletproof window. Back home, I'd help Grandma coat the fish with cornmeal and fry it in her cast-iron skillet. After dinner, she'd never wash the skillet. She'd pour some of the oil into an old Chock full o'Nuts can and let the rest live in the pan. The years of grease and love gave her food an original flavor that, to this day, no one can match.

Who was happier, Eddie in Brooklyn or Lennie in Manhattan?

I never really thought about it. Both places were full of character and had their own authentic vibe. I would have been stimulated by either borough. But living in two at the same time only served to overstimulate me. I leaned in and explored all the extreme interests and thoughts inside me. I saw that I could find adventure anywhere.

Take our swanky Upper East Side neighborhood. Some saw it as stuffy or snobby. I saw it as a beautiful tableau, almost like an amusement park. A few steps from our front door was Fifth Avenue, where, at the entrance of the Metropolitan Museum of Art, crowds were always congregating: tourists, locals, school kids, hot dog vendors, postcard vendors, acrobats, caricature artists, roller skaters, and mimes. One of those mimes, I recognized years later while watching *Mork and Mindy*, was Robin Williams.

In the other direction was Madison Avenue. I can't imagine two more different streets than DeKalb in Bed-Stuy and Madison Avenue in Manhattan. DeKalb was funky; Madison was fancy: block after block of boutiques and bookshops where I could leaf through *Peanuts* and *Curious George*; antique stores and art galleries with strange objects and gorgeous paintings in the windows; French bakeries with crepes and pillowy croissants.

After I finished preschool at Junior Academy in Brooklyn, the script flipped. From then on, I spent the entire week in Manhattan and only weekends with my grandparents. That's because my folks had enrolled me at Ethical Culture on the Upper West Side for kindergarten and then first grade at Public School 6, just a block from our place. Because our neighborhood was super-affluent, P.S. 6 had the feeling of a progressive private school. It was an education and an awakening in every sense.

On my very first day of school, a kid bolted from out of nowhere, pointed at me and my parents, and yelled, "Your mother's Black and your daddy's white!" Before that moment, I had never thought about my parents' skin tones. They were what they were. What difference did it make? Who cared? What was the big deal? The kid's accusation made no sense to me, but it did get me thinking. I was being ostracized, and I had no idea why.

When I got home that day, Mom knew something was wrong. She also knew that kids have a hard time expressing their feelings. That's why, years before, she had introduced a game where she became a character named Ruff Ruff, a magical dog. Ruff Ruff was a friend I could tell anything to. He was my mother's way of getting me to express pent-up feelings.

The game began with Mom asking to me say "Abracadabra." When I did, just like that, she became Ruff Ruff. Ruff Ruff wanted to hear whatever was on my mind, all the bad things that might have happened during the day, all my fears, all those nightmares about being trapped in a grave. Ruff Ruff would nod or smile or laugh. Ruff Ruff always understood me. Ruff Ruff kept my secrets. Ruff Ruff always made me feel better. To get Mom back, all I had to do was say "Abracadabra" again, and there she was. Roxie Roker was a gifted actress, mother, and empath who understood how to combine all three roles.

Outside the Ruff Ruff/little Lennie dialogue, my mother had her own viewpoint on race. She knew it wasn't enough to just let me vent my feelings when some kid called me a zebra. She realized an explanation would be needed. And her explanation was simple: I had two heritages, one Russian Jewish and the other African Caribbean, and I should be proud of both. At the same time, she made it clear that the world was always going to see me as *only* Black. To the world, my skin would be my first and only identification. I accepted her explanation and didn't object. If that's the way the world saw me, fine.

Then, and now, I proudly identify as Black.

Dad was also proud to have a Black wife and son. He not only loved my mother, he adored Grandma Bessie as well. He was closer to his mother-in-law than he was to his own mom. He also had great respect for his father-in-law. The two men were tight.

The conflict was never between Dad's and Mom's folks. It was between Dad and me. His military training defined him. And he was determined to put that on me. He commanded me to make my bed every morning so perfectly that he could bounce a quarter off it. He tormented me if there was a single book, toy, or article of clothing out of place.

I was just a kid. I never matched up. He was constantly unhappy with me. Yet there were many sides to Sy Kravitz. While he was rigid, he was also rich with charisma. He had the gift of gab. He could talk to *anyone*. He made people comfortable.

When I was still a toddler, we started traveling upstate as a family to visit my dad's daughters. I was excited to discover I had sisters, and they were as happy to meet me as I was to meet them. Laurie, Tedi, and I quickly fell into a rhythm, and we became family—all thanks to the gentle strength of Roxie Roker.

And how's this for true elegance? My mom insisted that when we went on trips to the Bahamas my sisters come as well. She was going to blend this family if it was the last thing she did—and she did. The bond among the various members of my parents' families grew deeper than anyone could possibly have imagined. My grand-parents Joe and Jean Kravitz had turned a cold shoulder to Roxie at first. But it didn't take them long to realize that the Rokers were extremely special—kind, generous, thoughtful. Sy's folks soon grew to treasure Mom's parents, and vice versa. It was a massive lesson in letting love conquer hate. Beyond bias was incredible joy. And many years later when Roxie had the means, she sent money and gifts throughout the family on an ongoing basis, making sure every-one was taken care of.

Grandma Jean and Grandpa Joe lived at 3311 Shore Parkway in Sheepshead Bay, Brooklyn. Here was yet another universe, Old World energy: kosher butchers, delis, synagogues. Like Dad, Grandpa Joe had his charms. He was well groomed and a sharp dresser. He had the gold chain with the *chai*, the sapphire pinky ring, and he smelled of cologne. Though he was in the *shmata* business, he wanted to be an entertainer to the point that he actually commissioned an oil painting of himself wearing a tux and singing into a microphone. He saw himself as an Al Jolson or an Eddie Cantor, Jewish singers who hit the big time in mainstream American music. That portrait hung in the entryway to their apartment, but Grandpa Joe never made it into show business. Instead, he became a tailor, which he claimed was the meaning of the name "Kravitz."

Unconsciously, I think he nudged me toward his deferred dream. He was the first person to put a microphone in my hand. Grandpa owned a reel-to-reel and loved recording himself singing show tunes. When he got tired, he'd turn it over to me. He taught me songs from *Carousel* and *South Pacific*. I picked up the vibe and jumped right in. It was natural, and it was fun. And when the music died down, Grandma Jean kept the party going by teaching me *durak*, a Russian card game whose name translates to "The Fool." We'd play for hours while I devoured her chopped liver on matzo.

Beyond the portrait of my grandpa, the centerpiece of my grand-parents' apartment was an oil painting hanging over the fireplace in the living room. A beam of light shone down on the face of a handsome young man. He was Leonard Kravitz, my dad's younger brother, who was killed in the Korean War at twenty years old. For sacrificing his life in the protection of his entire platoon, he'd eventually be awarded a posthumous Congressional Medal of Honor. As a young kid, I couldn't keep my eyes off this painting, this shrine to a fallen son. I felt the great weight of the loss and heartache over my namesake.

That pain was the root of the resentment Grandma Jean had for my father. Dad had been the first to join the armed forces, prompting his younger brother to follow suit. I think Grandma was convinced that if Dad had not enlisted, Leonard wouldn't have either. In her mind, my father was a cause of Leonard's death.

I also felt a bitter tension between my father and Joe. It was not until many years later that my mother explained the source of that tension. Grandpa Joe was not a faithful husband. Dad despised how his father cheated on his mother. Back then, I didn't have a clue about these grown-up concerns. I was just a happy-go-lucky kid hanging out in my grandma's kitchen eating kasha varnishkes. When I became an adult, though, and started watching Woody Allen movies, I recognized my family on the screen. That was the Jewish humor that raised me.

In 1969, Dad went to Vietnam as a journalist and Army Reservist. He was gone nearly a year. I remember seeing pictures of him from Saigon. He was holding a camera and a machine gun. He would tell stories of how much he loved Vietnam—the people, the food—and how he had his own house and a maid.

Part of me was relieved that he was gone. The heaviness lifted. Dad ruled the roost. My mother's old-school Bahamian upbringing taught her to defer to the man of the house. So, she didn't question his authority. At the same time, Mom was no pushover. She enforced her own tough brand of discipline, making sure, for instance, that I did my household chores. But unlike Dad, she enforced with love. Dad enforced with fear.

When Dad finally arrived home from the war, Mom was happy. I was conflicted. He immediately reestablished his role as Enforcer. Part of me was grateful that he was back. But another part of me hated how he was already back on my case: *Why are those socks not put away? What are all those Hot Wheel tracks doing in the middle of the floor?* When Dad returned, tension returned with him.

Bed-Stuy was a welcome escape from that tension. The crazy thing is that these two living situations, though radically different, balanced me. I can't say they forced me to adapt to any situation, or if I was born with that ability. But I can say that when it was time to go to Brooklyn, Eddie ran.

It was in Brooklyn where Grandma Bessie first started musing about my musical talent. It began at the Waldbaum's supermarket on DeKalb Avenue. She was paying for her purchases and I was standing next to her when I started singing a melody. The cashier recognized it as Tchaikovsky. He wanted to know how in the world this little kid knew Tchaikovsky. Surprised, Grandma turned to me for the answer. I said it was something I'd heard on my Show 'N Tell, a plastic TV with a record player on top. It was a melody that had stuck in my head. The cashier told my grandmother it was a highly complicated melody for a child to memorize. I just shrugged. It didn't seem like a big deal.

Broadway show tunes, pop songs, symphonic themes—they all stuck in my head. They gave me pleasure. But there's a difference between pleasure and passion. Musical passion didn't really kick in until the Jackson 5. The J5 were the game changer. They came storming out of the gate in 1969, when I turned five, the same year I was haunted by those stuck-in-a-tomb nightmares. Their early run of smashes—"I Want You Back," "ABC," The Love You Save"—had me mesmerized. Those hits opened my mind and heart in a way that no other music had ever done. It's one thing to say you like a band; it's another to say that a band changed your life.

LENNIE JACKSON

S ome called the Jackson 5 bubble gum music. It was anything but. Their hits were complex melodies and sophisticated arrangements. Even as a kid, I recognized that: the bass lines, the rhythm guitar, the percussive nuances. But beyond the music, they wore brilliantly patterned psychedelic-styled clothes and executed pinpoint-precise super-sharp choreography. At the center of it all was Michael. He was eleven but looked younger. I related to him.

In my parents' apartment, I had already been listening to great voices coming off their records. Mom and Dad loved soul music. I knew Aretha Franklin, Gladys Knight and the Pips, Al Green, Curtis Mayfield, Otis Redding, and all the others. That's why I can say that I knew that Michael, even at his young age, was as great as the greatest.

When I listened to the Jackson 5, I'd follow the conversations among the brothers and their musicians. I was right there. I heard how Michael was responding to the rhythm section. I understood how all the elements hung together—the strings weaving through the funk, the harmonic punctuations of the brothers' background vocals, Michael's lead vocal sailing over the top.

My response to their music was instinctual. I'd run to the closet, put on my black rubber galoshes (which I pretended were leather boots), drape myself in a few of Mom's scarves, grab a Magic Marker to use as a microphone, and join the lineup. Mimicking the brothers' moves, I became the sixth Jackson. At school, this is what I wrote in my notebook:

Lennie Jackson
Lennie Jackson
Lennie Jackson

•

It was October 16, 1970. I was six. I was surprised when Dad met me at school that day and said he was taking me somewhere. We walked a block over to Fifth Avenue and my dad hailed a cab. He told the driver, "Madison Square Garden."

I asked him, "What's at Madison Square Garden?"

In my mind, I was thinking, *Is it the circus? The Ice Capades?*

He wouldn't say.

I became uncontrollably curious. The more I asked, the more he wouldn't say. All he did was smile back at me with a sparkle in his eye. I had seen my dad happy and charming around his friends. But this was a first. Never before had I felt him this happy around me and me alone. When we finally got out of the cab and walked toward the Garden, my curiosity reached a boiling point.

The Garden was packed, everyone dressed to the nines. Men in leather maxi coats. Women in hot pants. Afros, wild hats, turbans, dashikis—you name it. Soon, as we settled into our seats, which were really close to the stage, a massive commotion broke out. The Queen of Soul was entering the arena. Flashbulbs popped. Heads turned. People cheered. Aretha Franklin, swathed in white mink and dripping in diamonds, had entered the arena. She and her entourage took their seats right behind us. Even before the music started, even when I still didn't know who we were about to see, the proximity of the Queen gave me goosebumps.

Moments later, the lights dimmed. A band came onstage and started playing. It sounded good. I started moving. I had no idea who they were. It didn't matter. I loved hearing live music, and I was happy to be there. When they finished, I thought the show was over. My dad laughed and told me, no, that was just the opener. (I'd later learn that the group was the Commodores, before they were called that.)

I could feel a restlessness in the air. People started clapping and stomping their feet. What's going on? All of a sudden, the lights dimmed again. Blinding spotlights exploded to life. I could make out a bunch of guys running onto the stage and taking their positions. And then it happened.

Bump.

Bump-ba-da-bump.

Ba-da-dum-badah-dah.

Bum-bum-bum-bum.

Bum-bum . . . BUMP.

All of a sudden, I realized I was looking directly at the Jackson 5 as they launched into the intro of "I Want You Back." I couldn't believe it. It was a million times more explosive live than it was on my record player. The vibration pierced me to my core. There I was, in front of my real-life heroes. Their moves were precise, expressive, and irresistible. They were flawless. And Michael's soulful, angelic voice soared. It was surreal. I jumped out of my seat. This was the best moment of my life.

The Jackson 5 were touring behind their *Third Album*, a record that had come out only a few weeks earlier. I already knew it by heart. I especially loved the James Jamerson bass line to "Darling Dear," a song never released as a single. The hits "I'll Be There" and "Mama's Pearl" were dynamic. The album cover mesmerized me. I used to stare at their faces, their perfect Afros merging into one another. Their look inspired my Afro.

During the show, Dad pulled out his Leica. Being a photographer and realizing what this night meant to me, he documented it. To this day, a photograph from the concert remains on my wall and is one of my most prized possessions. It documents more than a life-altering event. It documents my father's love and understanding of who I was. It's interesting how much he missed about me, how much space there was between us. But at that miraculous moment in time, his insight lit the spark. That spark would define who I would ultimately become.

On the taxi ride home, I dozed in and out of sleep, leaning on Dad's arm. Never had I felt so close to him.

Though he cared for me, Dad didn't really understand how to deal with me. On a Sunday morning not long after the Jackson 5 concert, he took me to Central Park to watch me ride my bike. He sat down on a bench and I took off. Everything was going fine until the front tire hit a rock, and I crashed. My jeans ripped and my knees bled. I started crying—and got Dad angry.

"If you don't stop crying," he said, "I'll give you something to really cry about."

I didn't understand his anger. Was he mad because I'd fallen or because I was crying? Instead of consoling me, he grabbed me by the arm and rushed me home. When we got there, he told Mom that she had a crybaby for a son.

Rather than argue with her husband, Mom waited till bedtime before asking if I wanted to say the magic word. I did: "Abracadabra," and suddenly Ruff Ruff was right there for me. Ruff Ruff patiently listened to me. Ruff Ruff heard my confusion. Ruff Ruff understood how embarrassed I was. Ruff Ruff took away my pain.

That same year, my parents took me to the Rainbow Room, on the sixty-fifth floor of Rockefeller Center, in the midst of Manhattan's glittering skyscrapers, to celebrate my sixth birthday. Duke Ellington was playing that night, his orchestra outfitted in formal tuxedos, looking like diplomats. Duke was dressed in white. The sound of his big band was enormous. Mom and Dad knew Duke, who came to our table for a brief moment. The great man picked me up and conducted his musicians as they broke into "Happy Birthday." Saxophonist Paul Gonsalves walked over and played the melody right in front of me. Even though he didn't know how to show physical affection, enlisting Duke was Dad's way of making me feel special.

Other men were openly affectionate. Take Sid Bernstein. He was my friend Adam's dad. Sid was the promoter who'd brought the Beatles to America and publicized their legendary concert at Shea Stadium. Sid worked with everybody, from James Brown to Herman's Hermits.

You could fit our tiny apartment into one of the walk-in closets of the Bernsteins' fifteen-room spread at 1000 Park Avenue. Each of the six Bernstein kids had their own bedroom and a private bath. The family dining room was as long as a bowling alley. Framed gold records lined the walls. There were nannies, cooks, and housekeepers. And then there was Sid himself, a big, loving man who took us to Patsy's Pizzeria in Harlem, where he could devour three whole pies. Sid was full of life, full of fun, and free with his emotions. Every time he greeted his children—me included—he gave us bear hugs and kisses. It was the kind of affection from a father figure that I really craved.

Whatever my father lacked, he did do wonderful things for me. When I was seven, Dad took me to Manny's Music on Forty-Eighth Street and bought me my very first guitar, a Yamaha acoustic with a built-in pickup with volume and tone knobs on the front. He also bought me a little practice amp. I'd been studying the Fender catalogue for months and was dying for a curvy sunburst Stratocaster. But Dad explained that this guitar was a more versatile way to start. I couldn't complain—and didn't.

My first attempt to actually write music came through my friendship with a guy who lived across the street from me, Alex Weiner, a lanky kid with long hair. Alex's family had this cool apartment that belonged in Greenwich Village, not the Upper East Side. His mom was a hippie who believed in artistic freedom. The atmosphere in the Weiner home was moody. Some walls were painted black, some covered with scrawling graffiti. Alex's mother actually encouraged us to paint on the walls. I loved this place! Better yet, Alex owned the exact Stratocaster I was dreaming of, and a Fender amp. Together we wrote something called, "I Love You, Baby." At that age, what did I know about love? But I did know that "love" needed to be in the lyrics.

We might have written the song on a contact high because Alex's apartment always smelled of marijuana. That aroma wasn't new to me; it was all over Bed-Stuy, too. It was also a fragrance present at the parties my parents took me to as a kid. Mom and Dad didn't smoke, but a whole lot of their friends did.

Pot seemed harmless, but that wasn't true of other stimulants. I watched a mother of a close friend waste away on prescription drugs. They lived in an enormous apartment at 1010 Fifth Avenue, a landmark building off Eighty-Second Street, just two doors away from us. Their place was a disaster: plates piled high in the sink, dirty clothes scattered all over the floor, trash cans overflowing. When I told Mom about it, she rushed over to investigate and ended up washing dishes, mopping floors, and opening up windows to let in fresh air. She even bathed the poor woman and put her in fresh clothes. She convinced her to get professional help. That was my mother: a rescuer of lost souls.

Mom loved music as much as I did. Two of her prized albums, *Imagination*, by Gladys Knight and the Pips, and Stevie Wonder's *Innervisions*, became childhood landmarks. I used to love performing Gladys's record for my mother. I'd sing along to "Midnight Train to Georgia," and she'd sit attentively and watch every move. She'd let me get through the whole album and never once take her eyes off me. Even today, a half century later, the beautiful warmth of Gladys's tone comforts me. Gladys gives voice to my mother's soul. Mom's soul and Gladys's voice are forever linked in my heart.

Stevie's album was a revelation. It was the first suite of songs I listened to where I focused on each overdub as a separate entity. This was my first conscious introduction to the meaning of a musical arrangement. Even as a kid, I saw *Innervisions* for what it was: a work of great art. There was a technical marvel to the whole operation.

Beyond appreciating the intricate construction of each song, I was breathing in Stevie's spirituality. Later on in my life, as I listened to this album again and again, I visualized Stevie sitting in the palm of God's hand.

In the summer of 1973, Mom and Dad sent me upstate for two months to Lincoln Farm, a sleepaway camp in Roscoe, New York. I brought my Yamaha, and one of the counselors who played guitar taught me how to play songs like John Denver's "Take Me Home, Country Roads." Not wanting to be left out, I also joined the camp marching band. When Mom and Dad showed up on Visitors' Day, there I was, playing acoustic guitar in a marching band. That had to have been a first. Mom and Dad called it the funniest thing they'd ever seen.

Once I was home from camp, Mom sent me to the Harlem School of the Arts for guitar lessons. I was nine. She taught me to ride the bus by myself up Madison Avenue and into Harlem. I loved that feeling of independence, and I was happy to be playing my guitar. I have to say that I wasn't a natural when it came to reading music, but I could follow by ear. My ear always has been and always will be my saving grace.

ISLANDS AND ANCESTORS

BAHAMIAN RHAPSODY

Manhattan and Brooklyn—the first two locations that formed my character.

Then came the Bahamas.

They were, of course, Grandpa Albert's roots. But once I saw them, once I felt them, once I breathed in that island air, they became my roots, too.

The first trip was the most thrilling. It was Christmastime. I was five. I woke up in our New York apartment, looked out the window, and saw that it was snowing like crazy. Mom had all the suitcases packed, and off we went! We took a cab through the storm to JFK for our flight to Nassau. In those days, air travel was not treated casually. You dressed up. Always properly attired for every occasion, Mom wore a bright blue ensemble. Dad was in a suit and tie. I had on a little sports coat and matching pants.

Passing by the TWA terminal was an adventure all its own. The building was straight out of *The Jetsons*, a futuristic piece of flying architecture designed by Eero Saarinen, with winged roofs and crazy-angled windows looking over the runways. Then, arriving at the Pan Am terminal, I saw our 707 as a time machine. Mom strapped me in my seat. My heart was hammering as we lifted off, piercing the clouds, climbing over the weather, watching the blanket of gray dissolve into radiant blue. I drank soda and flipped through *Archie* comic books. Dad read the *New York Times*. Mom studied her scripts.

Then, three hours later, the giant bird landed on an island bathed in sunshine. When the smartly dressed stewardess opened the door, a flood of sweet air filled the cabin. It was humid and smelled like flowers. We walked down the stairs, onto the tarmac, and into the terminal, where a steel drum band greeted us with welcoming sounds. The grooves were soft, the feeling relaxed. Mom's cousin Esau, a handsome, laid-back Bahamian, was there with his twelve-year-old daughter, Jennifer: our beautiful Nassau family.

Sometimes Mom and I made the trip alone; other times, it was a bigger outing: Dad; Grandpa Joe and Grandma Jean; my sisters, Laurie and Tedi; and of course Grandpa Albert and Grandma Bessie. I also spent many summers there alone, living with Esau, Jennifer, and Esau's mother, who we affectionately called Roker.

That first time, though, when it was me, Mom, and Dad, we stayed on Paradise Island. Nowadays, Atlantis has turned it into a Disneyland-like resort. But back then, it gave off an authentic old-school vibe. We checked into the Britannia Beach Hotel, the last holdout of James Bond sophistication, where men in tuxedos and women in gowns gambled in the casino and hung out in the TradeWinds nightclub to hear Ronnie Butler and the Ramblers. Great musicians, from Count Bernadino to Trinidadian Mighty Sparrow, performed all over the island. Peanuts Taylor, a percussionist who had once reigned supreme at the Tropicana in prerevolutionary Havana, ran his own club, the Drumbeat, where half-naked dancers breathed fire. As a kid, I got to see that heady combination of music, flames, and flesh.

Nassau wasn't always paradise. The first time I stayed with Esau, I showed up with a huge Afro. Esau didn't approve. It didn't suit his conservative sense of style. Right then and there, he ordered me into the backyard and insisted that I sit on a stool. He then took a bowl, put it over my head, and sheared me like a sheep. I was enraged. But he was my elder, and I had been taught to obey my elders. Besides, I could never be angry with Esau for long. He was too beautiful a person.

Nassau had a way of relaxing people, even Dad. Once there, suit-and-tie Sy Kravitz changed his wardrobe to open-necked floral shirts and white linen shorts. He ate pigeon peas and rice, fried snapper and johnnycake. Esau playfully called Dad Conchy Joe, their name for a white Bahamian. Dad also let down his guard with me. In Nassau, I could almost do whatever I wanted.

One day, I watched my father and Esau hanging out on the docks with locals feasting on scorched conch, a Bahamian delicacy. They carved out the conch muscle, squeezed lime and sour (a lime-orange hybrid), and added hot bird pepper before downing it straight up (including the pistol, considered a potent aphrodisiac). The only other place I saw my father this happy was in Grandma Bessie's kitchen. In the soulful world of the Rokers, Dad lost that hard edge and found a mellow vibe that was missing from him in Manhattan.

Esau was an engineer at a communications company. He also managed homes for "snowbirds," winter residents escaping the cold. His own home was modest and spotless. His backyard was filled with mango trees. I'd climb those trees, pick the mangos, and eat them until I was bathed in sticky nectar. I'd spend days at the beach and nights at the Wulff Road movie theater, where I once saw a double feature of Bruce Lee flicks: *Fist of Fury* aka *The Chinese Connection* and *The Way of the Dragon*. The audience yelled at the screen at the top of their lungs. I yelled along with them. Bruce was my man.

In Nassau, you could go wild at the movies, but at home you minded your manners. In the Bahamas, I saw the origins of my mother's impeccable etiquette. It was "yes, sir" and "yes, ma'am," "please" and "thank you kindly." At meals, you sat up properly, no elbows on the table. And you spoke only when spoken to. Mom called it "Bahamian home training."

The training took. The manners stuck, as did a Bahamian accent. My mom was tickled when I started calling her "Mummy." Nassau became a third home. It felt as natural as Brooklyn and Manhattan. The Bahamas are in my blood. The older I got, the closer the bond. Those islands never stopped calling me. Never stopped nurturing me. Never stopped bringing me a peace of mind I've found nowhere else in the world.

GODFATHER

s soon as we returned to New York, that mellow Bahamian aura was gone. Dad was back in his world of news, business, order, and discipline. He never stopped yelling at me to clean up my room. I never lived up to his standards. To keep the peace, Mom encouraged him to start a tradition of father-son outings. They were never as warm and cozy as I wanted, but I still loved being with him. Like every boy, I just wanted to hang around my dad.

Our quality time looked like this: we'd start out around eleven by walking over to Lexington Avenue, where he'd get me an ice-cream cone of my choice before we headed over to a little store with a green-and-white marquee that read "OTB," for "off-track betting." While I sat in the corner, Dad scrutinized the *Daily Racing Form* before placing his bet. He was a serious gambler. I'd later learn about secret debts, but at the time I had no idea. I just thought he liked to play the horses. Seemed as wholesome a hobby as any.

Next stop, shopping. This ritual really pleased me. I got a kick out of having a handsome, stylish father. When the old Italian tailor fussed over him with chalk-striped flannel suits, my dad looked like a president or a king. And to top it off, he had his initials engraved on the cuffs of his dress shirts, every single one: *SK*.

On some of these bonding days we visited Peter Arnett, Dad's friend and fellow reporter in Vietnam in 1968, who later gained fame covering the Gulf War from Baghdad for CNN. Peter had married a Vietnamese woman named Nina, and it was in their apartment that I became pals with their son, Andrew, and daughter, Elsa. I learned how to use chopsticks there, while eavesdropping on Dad and Peter exchanging war stories.

Other days, we visited other buddies. Dad was able to navigate different worlds with grace and aplomb. One was this clean, crisp culture of journalists, television producers, and jazz musicians. The other was more mysterious.

Enter Uncle Vinnie, a character plucked right out of a Scorsese film. I never did know how he and Dad met. But it was clear that they liked each other and even clearer that Dad gave Vinnie infinite respect. As they really liked each other, Vinnie grew closer to me and my mom, too.

Sometimes we had lunch with Uncle Vinnie at Midtown Italian restaurants. Sometimes we visited him at home in Queens. Uncle Vinnie was enthralled by my mother. He respected her and appreciated her class and beauty. When she came along on those evenings, he went the extra mile to find the super-exclusive restaurant, the best table, the finest wine. When she spoke, he'd wait for the words to fall from her lips. He often brought her a gift, an Hermès scarf or a bottle of Chanel No. 5. She couldn't help but like him.

Uncle Vinnie made an impression. Big guy, salty New York accent, and always sweet to me. I liked his enigmatic aura. I also liked how he always put Dad in a good mood. My father got off on being around power. No matter the location, Uncle Vinnie held court, surrounded by huge platters of pasta and his entourage of cronies. I saw his importance when, during one of our lunches, Sammy Davis Jr. showed up, headed straight to our table, and, before greeting anyone else, kissed Uncle Vinnie on both cheeks.

Uncle Vinnie was a fixture in our life. His light shone bright, and his presence was as rooted as a tree. My father told me Vinnie was my godfather and that he would always have my back.

GODMOTHER

My mom blessed me with five godmothers. Without the presence of strong, beautiful Black women, I definitely wouldn't be who I am. Their positive and nurturing Black female energy came from the center of the universe. And that energy surrounded me.

I was an only child but never felt alone because my mother had carefully woven a close-knit group of the world's most impressive aunties. I cannot exaggerate the comfort I felt knowing that these forces of nature were looking out for my well-being.

First, Cicely Tyson. Before I understood the true depth of her glamour and her icon status, I knew only that she reminded me of my mom—something about their physicality and the way they both held themselves. Godmother Cicely felt like home, right from the first hug. She lived at Fifth Avenue and Seventy-Ninth Street. Roxie and Cicely were soul sisters. It was Mom who had replaced her in Jean Genet's *The Blacks* at the St. Mark's Playhouse. We never went to Godmother Cicely's apartment. No one did. She came to us. The fact that her place was off bounds to the outside world only added to her mystique.

I always looked up to Godmother Cicely, but it wasn't until I saw her in *The Autobiography of Miss Jane Pittman* that I realized her profound genius. I'd read about slavery in school and of course talked about it with my family at home, but I had never seen it reflected on-screen. And when I did, I was amazed, saddened, and then enraged. Even now, I can see the scene in my head as clear as day when the now-ancient Miss Pittman takes that agonizingly long walk to reach the whites-only water fountain. Epic.

Second, there was the brilliant Aunt Shauneille. Shauneille Perry and Mom had attended Howard together and studied at the same theater company in Copenhagen. Aunt Shauneille had a love and understanding of the arts that launched her to become one of the voices of her generation. She became a prominent director, writer, and actor, and her home at 444 Central Park West became a cultural mecca, the unofficial headquarters of the Black Arts Movement. On any given day, I'd be sitting in the corner of Aunt Shauneille's living room while Nikki Giovanni read her poetry aloud or ensembles rehearsed plays. I loved the drama. These artists were filled with energy and optimism—and Mom was in the middle of it all. Energy and optimism were two of her strongest traits. I studied at that school.

Aunt Shauneille's enormous living room housed a tall avocado tree, floor-to-ceiling bookcases, paintings, and gorgeous African masks that mesmerized me. Shauneille named her daughter after her first cousin, Lorraine Hansberry, author of the immortal play *A Raisin in the Sun*, who served as inspiration for Nina Simone's song "Young, Gifted and Black." The first African American woman to have a play on Broadway, Hansberry was one of the leading lights of our literary culture. She died tragically of pancreatic cancer when she was just thirty-four. Her namesake and I grew up like brother and sister.

Writer Toni Morrison was another close friend. She had gone to college with Mom and Aunt Shauneille, where they were part of the theater group the Howard Players. I have sweet memories of being in her home and playing with hers sons Dino and Slade.

Mom and Shauneille had been in the prestigious Negro Ensemble Company, along with Godfrey Cambridge, Adolph Caesar, and Al Freeman Jr. I watched my mother costar with Carl Byrd and Graham Brown in *Behold! Cometh the Vanderkellans*, and in *Jamimma* with Dick Anthony Williams and Arnold Johnson.

My mother never pushed me into acting, but she suspected I might have talent. Still, she was ambivalent. Shauneille was not: she cast me in a Christmas special she was directing, featuring Ossie Davis and Ruby Dee. I ended up going on to act in a Marx Toys commercial as well, where I played with a Johnny West action figure. And then my mom and I appeared as mother and son on a show called *Pets Allowed*.

In spite of these occasional gigs, I wasn't bitten by the acting bug. I didn't mind the attention, but I didn't seek it. My feeling for acting was nothing like my feeling for music. Acting would not direct the course of my life. Music was my true north.

My third godmother was Diahann Carroll. Aunt Diahann embraced her success proudly. As a triple threat—actor, singer, dancer—she became a Tony winner (the first Black woman to win Best Actress) and then a movie star. Then she broke ground with *Julia*, the first-ever TV series centered on a Black professional woman. Aunt Diahann married four times, as well as having a decade-long affair with Sidney Poitier. I was nine in 1974, when my parents took me to the premiere of *Claudine*, a Black-consciousness film that starred Aunt Diahann alongside James Earl Jones. Mom had a role in *Claudine*, too. I was on the edge of my seat.

Fourth godmother: Joan Hamilton Brooks in Los Angeles, Mom's oldest friend. The two had grown up in Bed-Stuy together, gone to Girls High together, and then both worked at NBC. Mom and Aunt Joan were joined at the hip. They would take the subway together every morning and run over to window-shop at Saks during lunch. They went to parties together and enjoyed the attention, but Joan was adventurous, more so than Mom. She liked living on the edge, and she could really sing. We connected. Later in my life, because Aunt Joan had such a youthful spirit, I could talk to her when I couldn't go to my mother. With her, I could really let my guard down.

Fifth, Joy Homer. She looked like a Hollywood starlet. Aunt Joy and Mom were girlhood friends as well, and they remained sisters until the end. When I was born, the first place we went after the hospital was Joy's, where we stayed for a week. Throughout our lives, Joy's home in St. Alban's, Queens, was an oasis. Countless weekends, Mom and I would take the Long Island Rail Road double-decker to Joy's house, a lovely Tudor with a pool. Joy's husband, Lee, owned a successful liquor store in Brooklyn, and they loved throwing lavish parties for family and friends. Joy was a character; she enjoyed her Benson & Hedges 100s and her crystal tumbler of vodka. Our stories would soon intertwine.

Cicely, Shauneille, Diahann, Joan, and Joy. Looking back, I think of them as a five-pointed star, and Roxie was there at the center. Their Black feminine energy is one of the reasons I've held on to my sanity through crazy times.

SAY IT LOUD,
I'M BLACK AND I'M PROUD

Black people have historically been underrepresented or misrepresented in the media. That's why my mom took me to every remote corner of New York City to find our people doing authentic artistic work. We saw plays, we saw dance, we read books, we heard poetry. Then came a new wave of Black movies.

In 1974, Aunt Diahann Carroll was coming out with her film *Claudine*. In it, she plays a hardworking single mother raising six kids. Claudine's boyfriend, played by James Earl Jones, is a garbage man. Together, they struggle to overtake the barriers of urban life. Their social worker is played by Mom. Gladys Knight is the musical voice of the story, singing soulful songs written by Curtis Mayfield.

I really related to Mayfield. His score for *Super Fly* cemented his hero status for me. My parents owned the gatefold album whose cover featured Curtis's face and, just below, the long-haired, white-suited Ron O'Neal, the "super-fly" Youngblood Priest—arms crossed, pistol pointed upward while sexy Georgia, played by Sheila Frazier, lies at his feet.

Like Marvin Gaye's *What's Going On*, Curtis's album was funky but subtle: Marvin moaning "Mercy Mercy Me," Mayfield embodying "Pusherman." The songs and films of that era were telling the real-life news. They were voicing the fantasies and frustrations of their fans.

Films like *Five on the Black Hand Side* dramatized the deep divisions in the Black community: the conservative, uptight Black father; the taken-for-granted, overworked Black mother; the rebellious daughter; the militant son. Stories of Black life intrigued me, especially those with a strong father-son conflict. I related.

I also was into movies like *Shaft, Sweet Sweetback's Baadasssss Song, Across 110th Street* (with a theme by Bobby Womack that became one of my favorite songs), *Hammer, Trouble Man, The Mack*—and songs like Stevie Wonder's "Living for the City," the Staple Singers' "I'll Take You There," Bill Withers's "Lean on Me," and the Pointer Sisters' "Yes We Can Can."

After seeing the Jackson 5, my second life-changing moment came when I was eight years old and Mom took me to the Apollo to see the Godfather of Soul, James Brown. We had all his singles and a half dozen of his albums at home, but they hadn't prepared me for the Apollo. Mom thought it was important that I have the experience, and, as usual, Mom was right.

We rode the subway uptown. Walking down 125th Street, R&B blaring from the record stores, we saw folks stepping out in their finest. I felt good all over. I felt even felt better when we got to our fifth-row seats. The air inside the Apollo was thick with smoke. The color of the curtains and the stage lights were dark magenta and rusty red. There was no stage set. Bare bones. When James slid out and hit with "Super Bad," the crowd got up and never sat down.

James never stopped moving. He wasn't creating rhythm; he *was* rhythm. He sang; he hollered; he fell to his knees; he did the splits; he handled the mic like a magician. He hit us with "Soul Power." He hit us with "Get Up (I Feel Like Being a) Sex Machine." Bootsy Collins, his new nineteen-year-old bass player, had a big, lopsided Afro. That was the coolest look ever. The whole thing knocked me out.

After the show, Mom and I got to go backstage: musicians packing up their instruments, technicians packing up their gear. We went right up to James's dressing room and peeked in. His shirt was off, his body covered in sweat, his hair all a mess. Mom waved hello. James waved back. She considered going in and introducing me, but the small room was already overcrowded. We walked out the back door and into the night, James Brown's music still ringing in my ears, my feet still moving. Harlem was alive.

As a preteen, I could take the A train by myself down through Manhattan, under the East River, and into Brooklyn, where I got off and caught the bus that dropped me off at Throop and Kosciusko. Manhattan was majestic, but Bed-Stuy was my bedrock. By the end of the week, I couldn't wait to get back to Brooklyn.

I'd go with Grandma to the houses she cleaned.

I'd go with Grandpa to the public library, where he'd check out an armful of books on history and philosophy.

I'd run the streets and hang out at block parties.

I also saw sex. The boys started early. Girls started having babies at thirteen. I caught my nine-year-old buddy Tommy humping a girl by the front door of his house. After they were through, he turned to me and said, "My dick needed something to eat."

I wasn't sure what that meant. I didn't know anything about sex. Years passed before I lost my innocence.

As a kid, my Afro was a big deal. It was a big part of my identity. In addition to the Jackson 5, it had been inspired by eleven-year-old singer Foster Sylvers, who had a hit record I loved. I couldn't catch the name when it came on the radio, but I memorized the melody. One Saturday morning in Bed-Stuy, I ran over to the record store on DeKalb Avenue and sang the song for the man behind the counter. He told me it was Foster singing "Misdemeanor." Then he showed me a publicity photo of Foster sporting a globelike coif so gigantic it practically covered his eyes. That's when I decided I had to out-Foster Foster. Though just a kid, I was Black and proud.

At the same time, I was a multicultural kid, too, and, like my Jewish cousins, I wanted to have a bar mitzvah. Mom and Dad had no objections. That's when I learned that yarmulkes weren't made for Afros; I couldn't get the thing to stay on my head! Also, as the only Black kid in Hebrew school, I felt a little out of place. The rabbis and the other kids didn't say anything; they didn't have to. Their looks said it all. I could almost hear them thinking, *What's this kid doing here?* I didn't stay long, and the bar mitzvah never happened.

But that didn't keep me away from Jewish tradition. Grandma Jean and Grandpa Joe always had us over for the holidays. I remember one Hanukkah celebration at a big social hall on Long Island. My cousins and I got ahold of a bottle of Manischewitz, snuck into a corner, and finished it off. At first all was fine, and when the party was over, my folks drove me to Bed-Stuy. That's when I started to feel funny. By the time I got to my grandparents', I was losing it. I went upstairs with Grandma Bessie, who put me in bed with her. I tried watching *The Waltons* Christmas special but couldn't focus. The room started spinning. Dizziness turned to nausea. I got up to change the channel, and before I knew it, I'd thrown up all over the television. That's when Grandma took me downstairs to the bathroom and put me on the toilet. It was coming out of both ends. It was a mess. I was sick for hours and spent the next week in bed. I never felt worse. I have never been drunk since.

MASTER LEONARD

One summer, Mom brought me to California to visit my godmother Joan Hamilton Brooks. Aunt Joan, along with her husband, Bobby, and daughter, Heather, lived in Santa Monica. My first impression of Southern California was positive. I liked the beach. What I liked most, though, was the music I heard at the Forum.

Seeing the Jackson 5 at the Garden was life-changing, as was seeing James Brown at the Apollo. But never before had I seen anything like Earth, Wind & Fire. The spectacle was mind-blowing. The songs—"Shining Star," "That's the Way of the World," "Reasons"— were monumental. The costumes were otherworldly: the band looked like alien kings from another planet. The polyrhythms, amplified by the pyrotechnics, intoxicated me. Even as a kid, I sensed that underneath the huge Egyptian symbols, the pyramids and icons, were hidden messages.

The EWF audience was more mixed than that for James Brown at the Apollo, but the funk was just as strong, the crowd just as wild. I loved watching Verdine White poppin' his bass while levitating over the stage. Verdine's big brother, Maurice, was the maestro. On his recordings, he seamlessly stacked multiple melodies: vocals, strings, horns, percussion, backgrounds. At the same time, his tracks never sounded choked. They breathed. How'd he do that? I'd have to figure it out. I spent years studying his techniques.

The opposite of the EWF experience were evenings spent with Mom and Dad at the sophisticated Carlyle Hotel, on the Upper East Side. Another family ritual.

On any given Saturday night, we'd take a pleasant stroll down Madison Avenue. Mom in a black cocktail dress, Dad in a dark suit, and me in a sport coat and bow tie. The Carlyle was an old-guard establishment where presidents, ambassadors, and movie stars stayed without drawing attention to themselves. To the right of the lobby was Bemelmans Bar, the walls decorated with illustrations by Ludwig Bemelmans, the man who drew the famous *Madeline* children's books. Then we'd proceed to our spot in the Café Carlyle, where Mom's friend Bobby Short held court.

It was an intimate space. The lights were dim. Women in pearls smoked Parliaments. Men in Brooks Brothers suits drank martinis. And Bobby was in a tux, complete with patent leather pumps with black satin bows, and no socks. "Now, that's chic," my dad noted.

Bobby called himself a saloon singer, but he was much more than that. He played piano effortlessly. His repertoire was vast. He had an encyclopedic knowledge of the Great American Songbook. He knew every tune Cole Porter ever wrote. He'd actually known

Cole. He also knew the history behind each song—what musical or movie it was written for and who first sang it. He was pithy and witty and the kindest man alive. Because he adored Mom, he made sure we had a ringside table. A pink spotlight caught his smile. He had an aristocratic bearing. He performed with such natural grace that even a kid like me—in love with the Jackson 5, James Brown, and Earth, Wind & Fire—learned to fall in love with songs written a half century earlier.

I wasn't crazy about the food at the Carlyle—it was too fancy and saucy—but I liked how the maître d' and the waiters called me "Master Leonard." After the first set, Bobby would make his rounds. The so-and-sos from Newport, the French Riviera, and the Amalfi Coast craved their audience with this extraordinary gentleman. They fawned over him as though he were the queen of England.

He'd wind up at our table, where he'd sit to catch up with the Kravitz family news. *What was Mom's next production? What story was Dad working on at NBC? Did we know that Nina Simone came by to see him last night? And what about you, little man, are you causing trouble at school or being a good boy?* He'd rub my head and say he saw me studying his piano playing. He knew that I loved music. "Next set," he said, "child, I'm goin' play you some funky blues, so you know I ain't no old fogey."

And he did. Bobby belted out bawdy Bessie Smith blues. I was still too young to understand the sexual innuendos, but I felt the raw rhythm. He performed a rendition of "Romance in the Dark" where he got up from the piano, turned his back to the audience, and began to grind and hug himself as if his arms belonged to a beautiful stranger we couldn't see. I was entranced. Bobby taught me that no matter how sophisticated the style or elegant the setting, soul is the bottom line.

Then there's the famous story of Mom and Dad taking Grandpa Albert to their usual haunt, the Rainbow Room, to see his idol Ella Fitzgerald. Ella had been told that a major fan was in the audience, so halfway through the set, when she started singing "Someone to Watch Over Me," she extended her arm to hold Grandpa's hand and began looking into his eyes. He froze. He was so nervous that he just stared at her like he was going to pass out. He couldn't even think to give her his hand.

After the show, Grandma Bessie was disgusted with him. "Albert," she scolded, "you finally had your chance with your girl, and you blew it."

That's the only time I can remember my grandfather speechless. At Mets games, for example, he wouldn't stop talking, shouting at the umps, cheering on his boys. Before we took off for Shea Stadium, I'd put on the Mets jersey Mom had customized for me. She'd stitched on "23," the number of Cleon Jones, my favorite player. These were the days of Tom Seaver and Rusty Staub. No matter the score, we stayed till the last out and left the game hoarse.

I also liked the game of chess, introduced to me by my friend Michael Lefer. I caught on quickly. I was never as good as Michael—he was training to be a pro—but I could hold my own. I joined a chess club, learned strategy, and developed my technique, eventually playing with a timer. It took a while, but once I understood the structure, there was freedom—like with jazz. Chess connected to the musical side of my brain. It was all about rhythm. *Think, move, click. Think, move, click.*

Grandma Bessie's game was bingo. She'd take me to her church, where I learned it wasn't as easy a game as it looked. That's because Grandma worked five bingo boards at once. She'd sit me by her side and claim me as her lucky charm. She won regularly, and as a reward for my patience once, she took me on the subway to the Radio City Music Hall Christmas pageant to see the Rockettes.

The cultural stimulation never stopped. Grandpa Albert, who loved classical music, kept his radio tuned to WQXR. He and Mom were always taking me to Lincoln Center to see artists like André Watts, one of the first African Americans to claim fame as a concert pianist. Then there was Stephanie Mills in *The Wiz*; Sherman Hemsley in *Purlie*; Linda Hopkins in *Me and Bessie*; Clifton Davis in *Two Gentlemen of Verona*. And always the biggest thrill of all: going with Mom to see Off-Broadway productions like *Dream on Monkey Mountain* with Roscoe Lee Brown.

Some sights I discovered on my own, mainly because the Metropolitan Museum of Art was just across the street. I loved racing my bike around the two fountains flanking the main entrance. Weirdly, the only time I got mugged didn't happen in Bed-Stuy, but right in front of the museum, when a couple of kids pulled a knife on me and stole my bike. But that didn't keep me away.

I took painting and sculpture classes at the Met. I roamed around the enormous galleries on my own. I gazed up at the statues of heroic warriors and horses covered in armor. I was there the opening day of the famous King Tut exhibit. I made little notes and sketches of things that caught my fancy, like Roman frescoes and majestic Renaissance landscapes and portraits, religious paintings that felt alive, often inscribed with a plaque reading "Volto Santo." I would chant it as I walked around: "Volto Santo. Volto Santo." "Holy Face." There was a huge exhibit called *From the Lands of the Scythians*, with glistening treasures from ancient Greece and the Middle East and all over the globe. I pretended it was my kingdom.

I'd have to call it a golden childhood.

"AND YOU BETTER NOT FUCK UP!"

Yes, I had those scary dreams. And I butted heads constantly with my dad. Yet it wasn't even close: the good times far outweighed the bad. I was one joyous kid.

Mom was the main reason for my happiness. Sometimes stern, always protective, she raised me right. Her main method was simple: she loved me with all her might. She spoke so gently and calmly that you can understand my shock when, sitting at the Brooks Atkinson Theatre at the end of a Broadway play in which she starred, I heard her speak words that I never would have imagined coming out of her mouth. I had no way of knowing then—and neither did Mom—that that performance would alter her life and the life of our family.

Mom was playing Mattie Williams, the female lead in *The River Niger*, a production of the Negro Ensemble Company written by Joseph A. Walker and directed by Mom's costar Douglas Turner

Ward. My mother received rave reviews, was nominated for a Tony, and won an Obie. And the play itself won the Tony that year. It was 1974.

At age ten, I was used to watching Mom perform. She was a consummate professional, flawless in all kinds of roles. But this was different. This time, she transformed herself into a woman with deadly cancer whose husband, an alcoholic poet, was at odds with their soldier son. The play reflected big issues: poverty, militancy, police brutality, the tension between Black matriarchy and Black masculinity. At the very end, the husband sacrifices himself for the good of his community. It is left to his wife, Mattie, to demand that the survivors carry out her husband's plan. And so, just before the curtain came down, my mom, as Mattie, rose up to shout, "And you better not fuck up!"

With that, the audience leapt from their seats and gave her a standing ovation. That would have been enough to create a memory to last a lifetime. As it turned out, though, behind the scenes something bigger was brewing.

Television producer Norman Lear was in the audience. This was when his show *All in the Family* was a national sensation. Lear was planning a spin-off featuring Archie Bunker's nemesis George Jefferson, played by my parents' friend Sherman Hemsley. Watching Roxie Roker on Broadway, Lear envisioned her as Helen Willis, a neighbor of the Jeffersons, which was also the name of the new sitcom.

A week or so later, Lear's office called to ask Mom if she was willing to read for the part. She was. Some friends warned her that TV would steal her soul. They looked down on situation comedies. But Mom was no snob. She was practical. Although an exceptional thespian, she'd never earned much money doing theater. This was an opportunity to make a decent living. Her father had raised her to be self-sufficient. She loved quoting the Billie Holiday song that said, "God bless the child that's got his own."

Besides, she respected Norman Lear. As it turned out, Lear respected her. When she flew to L.A., he attended her audition. On the spot, he offered her the role. But, he said, she had to understand a key element: she would be playing the wife of the first interracial couple in the history of prime-time television. Her character, Helen Willis, is married to a white man whom she'd have to kiss. Would that bother her? Instead of answering, Mom pulled out a picture of Dad. "This is my husband," she said. Lear smiled. The deal was done.

Back in New York, she said she'd have to return to Hollywood to shoot the pilot. I wasn't all that happy. Did that mean we'd be moving to L.A.? That was the last thing I wanted. I was about to go into sixth grade, the "senior year" at P.S. 6, the school I'd been attending for five years. Sixth-graders had the most status and the most fun. I also didn't want to leave my friends at school or my friends in Bed-Stuy. I didn't want to leave Grandpa Albert and Grandma Bessie.

Not to worry, Mom said. Lots of pilots are shot, but most never get picked up. There was an excellent chance this would simply be a one-time trip to the coast. She'd be back in a week. Let's just take it one step at a time.

That week, I was alone with dad. With Mom gone, all the good vibes were sucked out of the apartment. It was gloomy and gray. All Dad could do was get on me about every little thing. Without my mother, my mind was a mess.

When she came back, there was still no word on the fate of *The Jeffersons*. First, the pilot had to be aired. On the night of the premiere, Mom, Dad, and I, along with Grandpa Albert and Grandma

Bessie, sat on our living room couch and watched the show on our television set. It was great seeing my mom in the role. She was a natural. The part was made for her. I was proud. Half of me was rooting for the show to be picked up, while the other half was rooting for things to stay the same. I was dying to be a sixth-grade big shot.

It wasn't long before the word came down. The pilot was a hit. The audience response had been overwhelming. The network committed for a full season.

What did all that mean?

Mom said it meant that she and I would be leaving soon for L.A. Dad would join us later. I'd be going to school in California.

No time for reflections. No time for objections. Things were moving so fast my head was spinning. Excited, angry, anxious, curious—I experienced every emotion under the sun. Our life was being turned upside down. We didn't know what was coming.

SUNSHINE
AND SMOKE

MOVIN' ON UP

Where is everyone?

That was my first thought when I woke up in Santa Monica, walked out on the balcony of the apartment, and didn't see a soul. I could smell the ocean. I could see palm trees in every direction. But no one in sight.

It was 1975, I was eleven, and Mom and I were living at 2901 Fourth Street in the apartment of Aunt Joan; her husband, Bobby; their daughter, Heather; and Joan's mom, whom we called Sarge (short for sergeant). Everyone was afraid of Sarge, a bossy woman who could get Max, the family schnauzer, to piss and shit on command. Sarge was scary, but also lovable. At this point, Aunt Joan had gone rock 'n' roll. She sported a blond pixie cut and metallic thigh-high boots. She was space-age funky and looked like she belonged in LaBelle. Aunt Joan had come to love L.A.

I didn't. Santa Monica seemed desolate. I was used to the

sounds of honking cabs and roaring subways. The quiet was eerie. The Pacific was only a few blocks away, but I couldn't hear the waves or see the sand. I felt lost.

We were staying at Aunt Joan's because my mother wasn't sure that *The Jeffersons* would last more than a season. Always practical, Mom wanted to economize. That meant she and I slept on a pullout bed in the living room. I didn't mind. I was used to sleeping with Grandma Bessie. Besides, before we fell asleep, I liked helping Mom learn her lines. I played the other characters. When I read their parts too blandly, she'd say, "Put more feeling into it!"

It took me time to adjust to California. No friends, new culture, new everything. But Mom, the ultimate professional, hit the ground running. Though she was appearing weekly on a national TV show and had good reason to ego-trip, she never did. Hollywood never seduced her. She was a New Yorker through and through. She proudly wore a subway token on a golden chain around her neck. Mom was a worker among workers. She didn't know how to drive, and at this point, she had no interest in learning. Nothing wrong with mass transportation. She'd stand at the corner and wait for a bus to carry her the ten miles across Santa Monica into the mid-Wilshire District, where she'd stand on another corner and wait for another bus that took her up Fairfax Avenue to Beverly Boulevard, location of CBS Television City. The trip took ninety minutes, but I never heard Mom complain. In contrast, all I had to do was walk across the street to Washington Elementary School.

Before the move, I'd been bitching about leaving P.S. 6. And even though I was unhappy about saying good-bye to the two neighborhoods I called home, Bed-Stuy and the Upper East Side, I knew I'd have been even more miserable if Mom had left me in New York with Dad. In her mind, that was out of the question. She took full responsibility for raising me. Though she never said so, she understood that her husband, as much as she loved him, wasn't capable of giving me the attention or the affection I needed. I never felt, not for a second, that she considered bringing me along to Hollywood as a burden. Mom and I were an inseparable team. And if she had to act as a single parent along with fulfilling the heavy demands of performing on a weekly TV show, she'd do it and she'd do it lovingly.

Following Mom's lead, I learned the bus routes, and whenever I could, I'd go to CBS to watch her tape her show. This whole new world of behind-the-scenes television was fascinating and fun. It's one of the reasons, though I missed everything about New York, that I started liking L.A.

The show was taped twice on a single day—at 5 and 8 p.m., and the final edit would be a combination of the two performances. Each taping was an event. The excited audience would be ushered in, eager for the show to start. Then each cast member, introduced individually, would come out to a burst of applause.

Here's Ned Wertimer, as Ralph the Doorman!

Paul Benedict, as Harry Bentley!

Zara Cully, as Mother Jefferson!

Berlinda Tolbert, as Jenny Willis!

Mike Evans, as Lionel Jefferson!

Marla Gibbs, as Florence Johnston!

Franklin Cover, as Tom Willis!

Roxie Roker, as Helen Willis!

Sherman Hemsley, as George Jefferson!

And Isabel Sanford, as Louise Jefferson!

Isabel, the queen of the show, came out at the very end to receive her royal welcome, as the entire cast bowed before her.

The show itself was always fun. The audience was ready to laugh, and their laughs were loud. Inside that soundstage, the real world disappeared.

Mom embraced her role. Her character was pivotal. Helen Willis was a proud liberal eager to confront George Jefferson's bigotry. The comedic timing between Roxie Roker and Sherman Hemsley was pitch-perfect. No wonder *The Jeffersons* became a classic.

The first season was about the radical change in the Jeffersons' lifestyle. The theme song, written and sung by Ja'net DuBois from *Good Times*, said it all: "Movin' on Up." The Jeffersons were moving to the East Side, the fancy New York neighborhood Mom and I had just left. It was super strange for me to see the backdrop of painted skyscrapers that provided the view from the Jeffersons' make-believe apartment on a Hollywood soundstage. I'd been pulled from real New York to a fake New York where my mother was in the middle of a comedy about people bettering *their* lifestyle the same way Mom was bettering *our* lifestyle. The Kravitzes were movin' on up right alongside the Jeffersons.

Our real move up didn't happen until the show's second season. That first year was all about adjustment. Seeing my mother shine in this new setting helped ease the sting of being the new kid on the block. But for a while I floundered. My classmates laughed at my New York accent. I didn't even know I had one. They got a kick out of how I pronounced "hot daawg."

Then there was the fashion and the ethnic disconnect. In New York, I wore a pair of jeans, a T-shirt, and Converse sneakers. Blacks, Latinos, and whites were all mixed together. Now I was surrounded by a tribe of blond-haired blue-eyed boys with hair down to their asses and a string of puka shells around their necks. In L.A. it was all about Hang Ten and OP shorts and Vans tennis shoes, which was really confusing, because in New York we called them sneakers. In California, there were other new words being thrown around, words like *radical*, *gnarly*, and *dude*.

The musical mix was different, too. I dug Elton John and fell under the spell of the Beatles, but I wasn't used to rock 'n' roll radio. Fortunately, I discovered 1580 KDAY, a Black AM station that featured familiar funk and soul, and funnily enough it was the first place I ever heard Bowie. To me, David Bowie's "Fame" was as funky as anything by the Ohio Players. In fact, before I saw a photo of him, I thought Bowie was Black.

Like her dad, Mom made sure I stayed on a spiritual path. She took me to Aunt Joan's church, Unity by the Sea, on Fourth Street. The minister was a woman, Dr. Sue Sikking, who preached the progressive lessons I'd heard at Grandpa's Science of Mind churches in New York. Aunt Joan had a powerful set of pipes, and limitless range. Sitting next to her, I was moved by how her angelic voice sailed over the choir and filled the entire sanctuary. At the end of the service, we sang "Let There Be Peace on Earth." Then the entire congregation hugged. After the service, we walked over to Zucky's, a Jewish deli on Wilshire Boulevard, for pastrami on rye.

My ultimate adjustment to Southern California, though, happened not as a result of church or even Mom's TV show. It happened because of a specific and beautiful man-made object: the skateboard. Before L.A., I'd never even seen a skateboard, much less ridden one. Now the skateboard gave me that feeling all kids yearn for: freedom. In New York, I had been free to hop on buses and subways. Getting around there had been a breeze. Compared to L.A., New York actually felt compact; L.A. was spread out. New York was vertical; L.A. horizontal. And a kid in a horizontal city needs a horizontal mode of transportation. The skateboard was the perfect vehicle.

Also the coolest. The skateboard was king. Southern California was skateboard central. And, man, I was ready to ride.

Jeff Ho's shop on Main Street in Santa Monica was to skateboards what Manny's Music in Manhattan was to instruments. It was *the* hot spot for surfers and skaters. Ho was all about style; he was known for his colors and airbrushing. His boards looked like candy; you wanted to eat them. Like Popsicles, they faded from purple to green to orange to yellow.

I came on the scene at a huge moment. It was the birth of Dogtown and Z-Boys. Skateboarders were learning to move like surfers. A hobby had suddenly become an art form. Wes Humpston was one of the pioneers of the movement. His little brother Mike, my schoolmate, brought a prototype of the Dogtown board to class. Little did I know that board and logo would become holy grails of skate culture. Wes was a visionary who turned empty swimming pools into practice fields. The dude became world famous.

I was on the sidelines. I never came close to becoming a champ, but the board let me smoothly glide into this new teenage culture. It let me adjust to California. It made me feel part of what was happening. But mainly it gave me mobility. I could finally move around. I took to it naturally. When I got halfway good, I could fly down the streets of Santa Monica, down to Venice, slide by the beach, and get where I needed to go in a hurry.

My first board was a Bahne with Cadillac wheels and Chicago trucks. An early classic. Eventually I moved to a Zephyr with Bennett trucks and Road Rider wheels, which now had precision ball bearings, making for an extra smooth ride.

I also got hooked on pinball machines. In my mind, pinball and skateboarding went together. Something about perpetual motion. I'd skate over to the arcade at the Santa Monica Pier and play those metal-legged monsters—Bally's Elton John Capt. Fantastic, KISS, the Rolling Stones—until my last quarter was gone.

The first season of *The Jeffersons* turned the show into a certified hit. The sitcom would run for eleven seasons and tape 253 episodes. Mom became a star. Her earnings grew far greater than my father's. This changed the dynamic in their relationship. It took me a while to understand the impact of that change.

On the surface, it was easy to see. Mom was getting far more attention than Dad. At the time, Dad seemed okay with it. He was his wife's biggest cheerleader. Her success made him proud and happy. But now that she was the bigger breadwinner, and not him, he had to adjust. For an alpha male like Dad, that wasn't easy.

Before the start of the second season of *The Jeffersons*, Dad left New York. He arranged to work at NBC News in L.A., and the three of us moved into a two-bedroom apartment down the hall from Aunt Joan. We were back to our same dynamic. More than ever, he was on me. In L.A., Dad was out of his comfort zone. In the light of Mom's stardom, he had to prove himself.

I graduated from Washington Elementary. Before starting John Adams Junior High in Santa Monica, I flew to New York to spend the summer in Bed-Stuy with Grandma Bessie and Grandpa Albert. It was so good to be back on the block. My grandparents always did wonders for my spirit.

So did Kevin Conner, a Brooklyn boy who'd been like a big

brother to me since I was five. He was eager to show me what was going on. One day, right there on the corner of Throop and Kosciuszko, where the Rokers had lived for forty years, a kid our age had set up amps and giant homemade speakers in his front yard. I asked him, "Why are you playing records outside?"

Well, the kid let me know that he wasn't playing records; he was making music.

I thought, *How are you making music with records? That's somebody else's music.* I didn't get it. He was mixing vinyl on two turntables. Then these guys who called themselves "emcees" started talking over the music. They weren't singing; they were telling stories over the recycled rhythms of songs I knew. This shit was *funky*. I loved it. Later, it would change my life and change the world.

With this music, a new style of movement was also born. The birth of break dancing was something to behold: I watched in amazement as guys in the neighborhood took sections of linoleum floors, laid them out on the sidewalk, and spun on their backs.

New York was being transformed visually, too. Subways were turned into canvases for underground artists. I liked the trains covered with graffiti more than the clean ones. The art spoke to me: fluorescent neon spray paint, whacky cartoon figures, flaming fireballs, ferocious snakes, and cuddly teddy bears devoured by slobbering green monsters.

I was witnessing the birth of hip-hop.

THE ZEN OF ZEP

ip-hop was a cultural game changer. But my own personal game changer came in two different forms. These forms collided my first year of junior high in Santa Monica. I'm talking about rock 'n' roll and marijuana. That combination propelled me in a whole different direction.

During lunch break, I jumped a fence and landed in an empty courtyard in a shuttered church. I was with Shannon Brock, who also happened to be half Black and half Jewish—only, in his case, his mom was Jewish and his dad was Black. Our other friend was a half-white, half-Hawaiian kid named Derek. He had a hippie dad who hung out with the Beach Boys' Brian Wilson. Derek and I loved riding our skateboards down Lincoln Boulevard to the Lucky supermarket, where he taught me to shoplift. Derek's family barely had enough to get by. This wasn't for fun. He was putting food on the table. He could slip a half-dozen steaks down his pants. I tried to

help him, but I was a rank amateur. The best I could do was walk out
with a box of cookies under my shirt. Mom, by the way, was crazy
about Derek. She saw his sweet side. Mom saw everyone's sweet side.

During our escape from school, in the deserted courtyard, Shannon broke out a joint, lit it, and passed it to Derek and me. I had tried
weed a couple of times before, but never felt much. For Santa Monica
teens in the mid-seventies, smoking weed was like breathing air. I
took a puff and exhaled. Still no effect. Shannon told me to hold it in
longer. I did, and this time something shifted. At precisely the same
time the head rush hit, Derek slipped a cassette in his boombox.

"Black Dog."

This was a moment. Maybe *the* moment. My head exploded. My
mind blew up with the sound of the screaming guitar, the crazed
vocal, the blasting beat. I was knocked on my ass. I hadn't even
heard of Led Zeppelin. I didn't yet know the names Robert Plant,
Jimmy Page, John Paul Jones, and John Bonham. All I knew was
that this music was electrifying every cell in my body. The mixture
of marijuana and "Black Dog" sent me soaring. The sky opened up.
The world got bigger and more beautiful. I was fucked up.

Shannon told me that I had to "maintain." *Maintain* was the
word. I had to maintain my high. Going back into school, I had to
find a way to act cool. It wasn't easy. When I tried to eat the leftover
lamb sandwich Mom had made for me, I couldn't chew or swallow.
When I walked into history class, it was like someone had turned
on a giant strobe light. Everything was moving in slow motion.
My teacher Mr. Richards gave me a pass to go to the bathroom. I
splashed water on my face, thinking that might bring me down. It
didn't. I looked at myself in the mirror. I asked myself, *Will I ever
come down from this?* I made a funny face. I smiled. I laughed. Even
though nothing funny had happened, I caught a case of the giggles.
Then came the munchies. I could have eaten a mountain of pizzas.

I went back to class, still high but able to hide it. On the first day of being stoned out of my mind, I learned to *maintain*, a skill that I would regularly employ for years to come.

On the same day and at the same time, I turned into both a pot-head and a Zep head. Before the end of the week, I'd bought every single Led Zeppelin cassette. Marijuana and rock 'n' roll became my steady diet.

Weirdly, Dad had prepared me for Zeppelin because of the Jimi Hendrix *Band of Gypsies* record he'd bought back when we were still in New York. That caught my ear but didn't set me on fire. Now with Zep ringing in my head, I heard their connection to Hendrix. Hendrix was the source. Turned out that *Band of Gypsies*, good as it was, was a live album and lacked the seismic impact of Hendrix's studio recordings. I dug deep into *Are You Experienced*, *Axis: Bold as Love*, and *Electric Ladyland*. Now I saw how Hendrix had opened the floodgates. He was *the* guitar god. Later, I learned that Jimi had been influenced by masters like Johnny "Guitar" Watson and Buddy Guy. As a kid, though, I heard him as the breakthrough genius. And it didn't matter that he had been dead for eight years. He lived inside my head. His rock rearranged my brain. I couldn't believe his intensity. Tonguing his Strat, smashing it against the sides of his giant Marshall amps, setting the thing on fire, distorting our national anthem in such a way that the song finally made sense.

Hendrix was rightfully the hero of every rock 'n' roller. But I had other heroes who were not accepted by the surf-skate culture of Santa Monica. I loved KISS, but my friends said that they were for fags and that the band looked like they were wearing Halloween costumes. I didn't give a fuck. As a matter of fact, on Halloween, I put on my mother's leotard, black tights, platform boots, chains from a hardware store, and a full face of Gene Simmons's demon makeup and proudly walked dead into the middle of the schoolyard.

Everyone thought I was insane. I thought I was the Black Gene Simmons.

I loved how KISS turned comic book characters into rock stars. I loved their theatrics. Front man Paul Stanley's androgynous allure, the way he belted out his bluesy riffs and pranced around the stage combining coquettishness with machismo. Ace Frehley's screaming guitar solos with his customized Les Paul smoking from the pick-ups. Peter Criss, the cool Catman with the perfect backbeat and the levitating drum kit. Gene Simmons's throbbing bass punctuated by his serpent-like tongue spewing blood!

I also loved the sophistication and slickness of Steely Dan. Walter Becker and Donald Fagen were brilliant musicians and storytellers who created a blues-based jazz-rock genre all their own. I could love both the most technically accomplished musicians—Weather Report, Mahavishnu Orchestra, Return to Forever—and still love KISS. One thing had nothing to do with the other.

Every Saturday, I was at the Guitar Center on Sunset playing every guitar in sight, plucking every bass, fingering every keyboard, pounding every drum set. Sometimes my mom would come along and patiently wait for me in the front of the store.

I was obsessed with sound, though I had no idea how to mix the sounds spinning inside my head. I'd hear a Stevie Wonder groove, a Hendrix lick, a Zeppelin riff, a Steely Dan *Pretzel Logic* story. How to put 'em together? Just keep listening. Listen to Bob Marley. Listen to the Eagles. Listen to Phoebe Snow. Listen to the Commodores. Listen to everything.

A lot of my friends came from hippie households. Hanging out in those beach bungalows did even more to connect me to an earlier era. Their folks openly did what we kids did in secret: smoke tons of reefer. Sex was still years away for me, but there were make-out parties with blond beach girls. Most of my friends' parents were in their thirties, as opposed to my mom, who was forty-six, and my dad, fifty-one. I listened to the grown-up hippies tell stories about hearing the Grateful Dead at the Fillmore West or the Doors singing "L.A. Woman" at the Whisky a Go Go. Their period posters of Canned Heat, Jefferson Airplane, and Cream made it seem like the summer of peace and love was still alive and well.

As opposed to our place, where Dad ruled with an iron fist, my friends' pads were loose and free. And lack of structure was just what I wanted. There, we could smoke weed, eat junk food, and watch cable TV for hours. Z Channel was the new thing. We could even sneak peeks of soft-core porn. Anything goes.

We could also blast the stereo as loud as we wanted. For my friends' folks, high on Acapulco Gold, the louder, the better. Seventies rock, funk, and four-on-the-floor disco. The Rolling Stones, Parliament-Funkadelic, the Bee Gees—I didn't discriminate. Cameo, Average White Band, Aerosmith, Donna Summer, Chic. All great.

Back home alone in my room, I kept honing my drumming chops. I followed Buddy Rich, who carried his seventeen-member band on his back. Buddy was a crazy technician. I studied all styles—rock drummer Keith Moon, funk drummer Clyde Stubblefield, bop drummers Max Roach and Elvin Jones.

I also heard the comics that provided the laugh track of my teen years. My friend Shannon turned me on to Richard Pryor. I put Pryor in the same category as Jimi Hendrix: the best of the best. Pryor was hysterical, but the hysteria was deep. He exposed everything. He said everything. He opened up his insides and offered them to the world. No one's ever been more vulnerable or more downright honest. *That Nigger's Crazy* was my jam. But so were all of Pryor's records. Me and my boys could do all his routines. His characters—Mudbone, the preachers, the pimps, the hos, the winos—were living, breathing people. I carried my dad's portable cassette player to school so we could listen to Pryor in the back of the library. He was taboo, and that made us like him even more.

The ultimate stoner kings were Cheech and Chong. Mom and Dad never did learn that I was a pothead. So to discover these pot-head comics, especially those who made the get-high ritual ridic-ulously funny, was like finding long-lost friends. Shannon, Derek, and I knew their routines by heart. Humor helped get us through school.

School was excruciating; if my teachers had made the material more engaging or applied it to life, I would have been interested. But it was all about memorizing facts, dates, and formulas. I came home with bad grades, and my parents were furious. They insisted that I focus. I didn't want to. Or, I should say, I was focused on other things. I just wanted to get high, play my guitar, and rock out.

Aunt Joan understood me, though. She was my godmother, but she became a friend. In fact, she started having more in common with me than she did with my mom. We would sit in her room and listen to Bowie while she modeled her new outfits for me. I thought she was cool. I didn't have to hide anything from her. She was my ally.

The second season of *The Jeffersons* was even more fun for me than the first. That season the show moved to Metromedia, in Holly-wood, at Sunset and Van Ness. That meant another long bus ride, but I didn't mind. I had the run of the place and was able to bring my buddies along; the security guards waved us in. That lot was my playground, and I knew every corner. The soundstages were as big as airplane hangars. Walking through the complex, I passed the set for *Good Times*, whose stars, Esther Rolle and John Amos, were family friends.

I saw how *Good Times* and *The Jeffersons* presented flip sides of the African American experience in the 1970s. One side was stuck in the ghetto, while the other side had escaped. *Good Times* was about being stuck. When I first saw the show's fake Cabrini-Green apartment in make-believe Chicago, it reminded me of the projects where my friends lived in Bed-Stuy. Meanwhile, *The Jeffersons* had escaped Archie Bunker's lower-class Queens and moved to fancy Manhattan. Working class and elite—both classes I'd known as a kid in New York; now both classes turned into comedies I was watching being taped in Tinseltown.

On the set of *Good Times*, I got to know Jimmie Walker of "Dyno-mite" fame and Ja'net DuBois. At *Diff'rent Strokes*, another show at Metromedia, I became friends with Gary Coleman, Todd Bridges, and Kim Fields from *Facts of Life*.

The Roxie Roker dressing room was my go-to spot. With Mom in makeup, I'd hang out, do my homework, and blast Stevie Wonder's "Boogie On Reggae Woman." Mom's world was chill.

Dad's, however, was not. After the move west, he had maintained his status as a news producer, moving from NBC to ABC, but what he really wanted to do was become a mogul; he wanted to make waves in show business. When that didn't happen, he grew frustrated. And I believe he took that frustration out on me. His fury about my grades grew and grew.

Mom wasn't happy about my grades either, but she understood what was going on. To keep things cool at home, she played down her prominence. Sensitive to her husband, she introduced herself as Roxie Kravitz, not Roxie Roker. When she learned to drive, she bought herself a plain old Buick and didn't complain when Dad traded in his Honda 600 for a Rolls-Royce that had belonged to actor Walter Matthau. She knew her newfound fame was tough on him.

Mom had no interest in social climbing among the Hollywood elite. Instead, she volunteered her time helping underprivileged kids at an organization called ICAN, the International Council for the Abused and Neglected. She also kept her theater roots, performing at the Inner City Cultural Center in Leimert Park. When it came to giving back, she was her father's daughter. She was also her father's daughter when it came to practicality. Grandpa Albert had taught her that middle-class people with a solid income owned homes. The Kravitzes had never owned a home—until now.

MOVIN' ON UP EVEN HIGHER

Moving from an apartment in Santa Monica to a ranch house in Baldwin Hills was a big deal. Our new home was a midcentury architectural gem, the kind of single-story glass-and-wood design reminiscent of Frank Sinatra in Palm Springs. Previously owned by a doctor, it had been featured in *Architectural Digest*. It wasn't a mansion—three bedrooms, a living room/dining room/den—but to me, a kid who'd grown up in a tiny apartment, it felt enormous. There was a pool in the backyard along with a greenhouse and avocado, lemon, and orange trees. The view was crazy. The house was situated atop one of the highest hills in L.A., and I could see the Coliseum, the Hollywood Hills, and a range of snowcapped mountains in the distance. The whole city was laid out at my feet.

The address was 4061 Cloverdale Avenue. Some called the neighborhood the Golden Ghetto. Technically, it was Baldwin Vista, a section of a larger area called Baldwin Hills. When we moved there in 1976, the original white owners had mostly taken flight, selling their homes to upper-middle-class Blacks. Stars like Ray Charles and bluesman Lowell Fulson were neighbors. Our house cost $300,000. On the white side of town, it would have sold for a million.

Baldwin Vista was perched at the highest point. Below us was Black, working-class South Central, whose main thoroughfare was Crenshaw Boulevard. We were six miles west of downtown and ten miles east of the Pacific Ocean—smack dab in the middle of everything.

Dad liked the neighborhood. And he and Mom saw "Cloverdale," as a perfect party house. Their parties back on Eighty-Second Street had been intimate and intense. But the Cloverdale parties were like scenes out of a movie. Late at night, with the lights of the city ablaze, my parents took pride in sharing their new home. There was Aunt Diahann in the living room laughing at something Flip Wilson had just said. Out by the pool, Godmother Cicely would be chatting with Robert Guillaume.

I had picked up my parents' gift for socializing. Accommodating people was their way of life; it also became mine. It wasn't calculated; it came naturally. Show curiosity about others, make them feel welcome, make them feel loved—that was Mom's way. And on party nights, Dad was easily the most charming man in the room.

I was a highly social teenager, but I had my issues. I was restless and excitable. I resisted all discipline other than the household chores Mom prescribed. I wasn't about to go against my mother. She reminded me that I had my own bathroom, which meant it was my job to scrub the toilet. It was also my job to clean the kitchen sink, my job to take out the garbage and do my own laundry. Come to think of it, I had to clean the whole house. Carpets had to be vacuumed. I had to wash my parents' cars before I could go out on weekends. If my friends were outside waiting for me, they were invited to help out, but I wasn't going anywhere until my chores were completed.

One night, Mom and Dad didn't get home from a party until 3 a.m. I was fast asleep. Mom didn't care; she shook me awake. I woke completely disoriented. She was furious because I hadn't done what she'd asked me to do. I said I had. I had cleaned the kitchen. I had washed the dishes, dried them, and put them away. She pulled me out of bed, marched me down the corridor into the kitchen, and stood in front of the sink and the cabinets. Nothing was in the sink! I had clearly done the job. But then my mother pointed to a cabinet whose door was barely ajar. She said, "Close the cabinet." I pushed it closed, and she said, "Now the job is done."

At the time, I thought she was totally insane. She'd actually woken me up in the middle of the night because a cabinet door had been cracked open half an inch. But that's how meticulous my mother was when it came to completing a task. Later in life, when I was deep into music projects, I kept going back to that incident and hearing her words, "If you do something, do it right."

I didn't have a problem with Mom's discipline. Maybe because her sternness was tempered with love, while Dad's was laced with anger, not to mention control. Dad seemed hell-bent on controlling me. At the same time, I had lots of freedom. That's because my parents were always off working. During the day, I had the run of the house. Friends came up to swim in the pool. Jam sessions went down in the living room and on the patio. I never stopped playing, never stopping trying to work up my chops on guitar, bass, drums, and keys. I also never stopped making music with my buddies in the Crenshaw District, a neighborhood called the Jungle, where the focus was on funk.

The upside to Cloverdale, its beautiful location high above the city, was also its downside. I was still enrolled at John Adams Junior High, and the ride from Santa Monica to Baldwin Vista took hours. I'd ride the Pico bus halfway across the city until I got to the corner of La Brea and Pico where I switched to the southbound 212. L.A. buses were nothing like New York buses. They didn't run as often.

I stood around. I paced. The air was thick with smog. The traffic was fierce. I smelled food from Lucy's Drive In, a burrito and burger joint. I wanted to eat, but had no money. I hated being hungry, hated waiting on that damn bus. When it finally pulled up, I jumped on, stared out the window, and started making music inside my head. I heard melodies without words. My hands beat out rhythms on the back of the seat in front of me. As the bus stalled in traffic, I fit the melodies on the grooves, singing to myself. The ride took an hour, but the music kept me happy. By the time I got off, my heart was singing. I passed by the Baldwin Theater where, stoned, I'd spend Saturday afternoons watching out-of-date films like *Blacula* and *The World's Greatest Athlete*.

Then I'd hike up the big hill to our house and get even happier when, after walking into my room and ignoring the mess, I'd pop in a cassette of KISS's *Hotter than Hell* or Steely Dan's *Aja* or John Coltrane's *Ballads*.

Like all good mothers of her generation, Mom was looking for ways not only to keep me off the streets but also to engage me in creative activities. She saw I had all this energy that needed to be channeled. Take acting, she said. Because I'm such an extrovert, she clung to the belief that I had dramatic talent. That's why she introduced me to her friend Whitney LeBlanc, who was directing a play called *Baker's Dream*, featuring Hal Williams, famous for his role as Smitty the cop on Redd Foxx's *Sanford and Son*. I auditioned and got the role of the son, Kevin. I memorized my lines, and in rehearsals, I enjoyed the creativity of these players I had watched on TV for years.

The play ran for a few weeks at the Apex Theater on La Brea Avenue. When I came out for curtain calls, the adulation from the audience felt great. Acting was fun, but it wasn't music. I didn't dream of becoming a professional actor the way I never *stopped* dreaming of becoming a professional musician. I also never dreamed that my childhood nightmare would give way to light.

SACRED AND PROFANE

My parents' wedding day with Grandma Bessie and Grandpa Albert.

Baby photo taken of me in Bed-Stuy, Brooklyn.

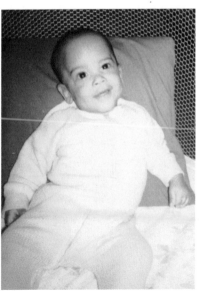

My first portrait.

With Grandpa Albert at Lincoln Center after church service. My mom is seated on the fountain behind us.

In the front yard of Grandma and Grandpa Roker's house on the first day of preschool at Junior Academy in Bed-Stuy, Brooklyn.

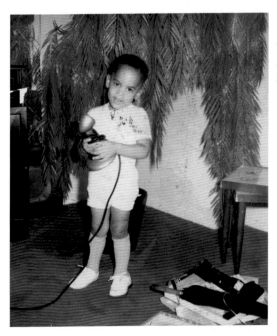

Singing into Grandpa Joe's tape recorder in Sheepshead Bay, Brooklyn.

In Nassau, Bahamas, with cousin Esau Roker.

At my birthday party at 5 East Eighty-Second Street with Grandpa Joe and Grandma Jean.

At 5 East Eighty-Second Street with my mom, Grandma Bessie, and Grandpa Albert.

On the stoop with my friends at 368 Throop Avenue in Bed-Stuy, Brooklyn.

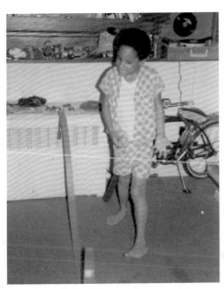

In my bedroom at 5 East Eighty-Second Street.

Backstage with my mother at the
Brooks Atkinson Theatre on Broadway
before a performance of *The River Niger*.

My fourth-grade class photo from Mrs. Goldberg's class at P.S. 6 in Manhattan.

My father took this photo when we went to see the Jackson 5 at Madison Square Garden.

Performing at Lincoln Farm summer camp in Roscoe, New York.

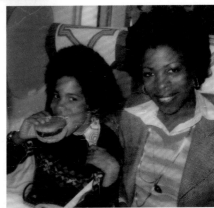

On the flight to Los Angeles with my mom for the taping of the first season of *The Jeffersons*.

Playing guitar for my parents at our apartment at 2901 Fourth Street in Santa Monica, California.

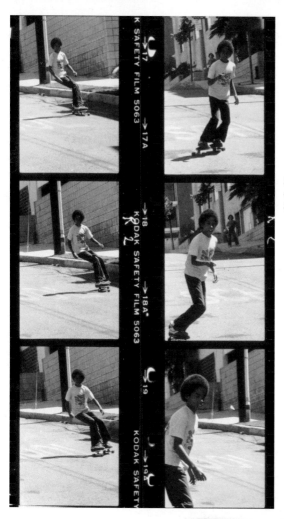

Skating down the hill
on Ashland Avenue in
Santa Monica.

Rehearsing for Mahler's Third
Symphony with the California
Boys' Choir and the Los
Angeles Philharmonic. To my
right is Noah Cotsen, to the
left is Phineas Newborn, and
two rows behind him is Joey
Collins.

LIKE ANGELS SINGING

W hat happened next transformed my life forever.

Through a friend from her New York NBC days, Mom heard about the California Boys' Choir. Knowing how much I loved music, she thought this could be an experience and an education. She took me to one of their concerts in Century City. I wasn't dying to go, but she didn't give me a choice. It turned out I liked the music. Forty boys sang with a beautiful blend. Their sound intrigued me. I enjoyed the intricacies of the close harmonies. I also liked their look: sharp navy-blue suits, white ruffled shirts, black velvet bow ties, and patent leather shoes. They were on their game. Afterward, I met some of the guys. There was a brotherhood vibe I really liked. When Mom asked if I'd consider auditioning for the choir, I surprised myself by saying yes. I could actually see myself up there singing classical music.

A week later, Mom drove me to the choir offices in the Museum of Science and Industry, near the University of Southern California. I was introduced to the director, Douglas Neslund, who sat at the piano, played a series of notes, and asked me to sing them. He heard that I had pitch. Then he played a melody and had me duplicate it. I passed the test.

Mr. Neslund told Mom I was good enough for the training choir. If I did well there, he said, I'd have a chance of making it into the concert choir. But before that, I'd have to learn to sight-read using an old Hungarian method called Kodály, which uses hand signs to represent musical notes. Because many of the choir selections were German, Italian, French, and even Latin, I'd have to master pronunciations completely foreign to me. Mr. Neslund asked if I was up to the work. I wasn't sure, but I said yes anyway. He reminded me that his standards were high. After the Vienna Boys' Choir, the California ensemble was the best in the world. Only accomplished singers were admitted.

Riding back home, Mom asked me if I thought I was ready for the grueling after-school lessons. She wanted me to go for it, but she also knew that in areas other than music, I was a poor student. But this *was* music. So I signed up. I liked the idea of joining a fraternity of kids my age who were serious about singing.

I followed through, spent months in the training program, and got admitted to the concert choir. That came along with a whole summer of more intensive training. At the end of that summer, we took the same entrance exam USC used to admit freshmen into its music department. And I was only twelve. Then we were ready for the concert season: symphonies, operas, recordings, etc. I discovered I had a real understanding and appreciation of classical music. My parents were proud.

My choir years turned out to be monumental. This was the only formal training in music I'd ever have. I didn't get formal training for R&B or rock 'n' roll. That was stuff I learned by feel. But developing vocal techniques under the supervision of exacting instructors was something that helped me forever. I learned to sing from my diaphragm. I learned breath control, enunciation, pitch. And I was thrilled to stand onstage with entire orchestras and breathe in the fullness of their sound as we sang melodies written centuries earlier.

Another big benefit was making lifelong friends. Choir buddy Phineas Newborn III had an advanced sense of music. His dad, whom he was named after, was a brilliant bebop pianist; his uncle Calvin was a great blues guitarist; and his godfather, Ray Brown, was the best jazz bassist in the world. Phineas was all personality—sweet, sharp, and witty—and without a mean bone in his body. He lived in Leimert Park, a Black arts neighborhood off Crenshaw, just down the hill from our house.

Phineas's cousin Joey Collins was also in the choir. Joey and his mom stayed in Baldwin Hills, close to Cloverdale. Like Phineas, Joey had beautiful energy and a big love of music. Those two became my brothers.

One day, Phineas and Joey were witness to an ugly episode.

A group of us choirboys were being driven home in our carpool. Mrs. Collins, Joey's mom, was driving, and Grandma Jean was riding shotgun. She had moved to L.A. after the death of Grandpa Joe and was now living in Park La Brea, a sprawling apartment complex filled with former New Yorkers, in the Jewish Fairfax District.

We decided to stop at Tower Records on Sunset. That was one of my favorite spots, a supermarket-size record store. While everyone wandered around, I meandered over to the KISS section. I spotted a bunch of their cassettes. Without giving it too much thought, I slipped one into my jeans pocket. It was so easy that I slipped in another. I looked around. The aisle was empty. This was a breeze. So, why not slip a third cassette into my shirt pocket, and a fourth and fifth into the back of my jeans, where they fit snuggly but securely against my waist. No one was in sight. I was set. I was cool. When I saw my friends and Grandma Jean heading out the door, I followed them.

The minute I walked over the threshold and into the parking lot, a hand grabbed me. I looked around and saw the mug of a massive security guard.

Busted.

My heart dropped to the ground. He took me to a back room, where a store manager said, "You've been caught red-handed. You do understand what this means. You'll be going to jail. This is serious shit. You have over sixty dollars' worth of merchandise. That's a major crime. You'll be kicked out of school. Your life is ruined. You've fucked up big time."

This rant went on for ten more minutes while I shook like a leaf. At the very end, just when I thought he was going to call the cops, he said, "I don't know why, but I'm giving you a break. I'm letting you go. But don't ever show your face in this store again."

I sighed the biggest sigh of my life. My relief was epic. I must have thanked the manager ten times. I was free to go, but since my friends and grandmother had seen me apprehended, there'd still be hell to pay. I had no doubt that Grandma Jean, who was absolutely furious, would tell Mom minutes after we arrived home. And she did just that. Thankfully, Dad was at work.

Mom was incensed. My conduct violated everything she stood for. My mother's moral code was simple: You never lied. You never cheated. You never stole. She sent me to my room, where I waited a good hour for her to reappear. She wanted me to think about what I'd done. I was ashamed and embarrassed. The longer I waited, the worse I felt. When she came through the door again, she had composed herself. She wanted to know why I had stolen the cassettes. I truthfully said because I didn't have the money to buy them, and I'd wanted them really badly. She asked if I knew how selfish and spoiled I sounded. Did I really think my life would fall apart if I didn't have those KISS cassettes? Did I understand how mortified she was to have raised a child who didn't understand the difference between right and wrong?

All I could do was apologize and promise it would never happen again. When she expressed her profound disappointment in me, her words wounded, but I was even more worried by what Dad would do when he found out. I'd be grounded for a year. But then, for the second time that day, I was given a pass.

"I'm not going to tell your father," Mom said.

WHAT?! I couldn't believe what I was hearing. I was in shock. My mother never hid anything from my father. That would have been against her code. But I guess she knew that if she told him, he'd go ballistic, and our relationship might not ever recover. The woman had serious ethics, but she chose me over them.

Musically, I was growing. I was absorbing an enormous amount of technical information that, in ways I didn't yet understand, would serve me even as a rocker. The performances were always exhilarating. They were my first live gigs. As a first alto, one of forty boy singers, I got a good taste of what it means to please an audience. Concert halls like the Dorothy Chandler Pavilion are musical temples with their own legendary vibes. You've got to deliver. Being part of operas like Verdi's *Tosca* or Mozart's *The Magic Flute* was surreal: the costumes, the contraltos, the high drama. I remember making our entrance in *Carmen*, and they actually had live horses onstage! Being in the pit with the symphony and singing along as the Joffrey Ballet did the Waltz of the Snowflakes from the *Nutcracker Suite* was a memory to last a lifetime—not to mention the ballerinas.

Nothing, though, could compare to our biggest concert: at the Hollywood Bowl. From the Beatles to Leonard Bernstein, the Bowl had hosted the best. That night, I dressed at home in my choir outfit then rode the chartered bus with Phineas, Joey, and my other choir mates. We were over-the-top excited. I couldn't wait to hit it. At the Bowl, we were led to the stage and shown our places. There we were joined by the Roger Wagner Chorale and the Los Angeles Philharmonic, directed by Maestro Erich Leinsdorf.

The Bowl is cut from the side of a hill. From the stage, I looked out at its tiered rows. There wasn't an empty seat: 17,500 patrons. The sun was setting. The stage lights went up. The first selection was the traditional hymn "Veni Creator Spiritus," "Come, Holy Ghost, Creator Come." Singing "Veni, veni, veni" blew my mind. I got goose bumps. Later, we sang during the fifth movement of Gustav Mahler's Third Symphony, entitled "What the Angels Tell Me." The Boys' Choir voiced the angels. The feeling was angelic. We were flying.

Backstage, Mom and Dad were waiting, all smiles, with—*surprise!*—Grandma Bessie standing next to them. I flew into her arms. I couldn't believe it. She'd taken a plane for the first time in her life just to see me perform. It was a beautiful night.

NIGHT OF NIGHTS

Beautiful is too weak a word to describe the next chapter of my choral experience. The right word is *epiphany*.

August 1977. That summer, I turned thirteen and went to the Boys' Choir summer camp at Loma Linda University, sixty miles east of L.A., where we rehearsed the repertoire slated for the new season. We weren't allowed to listen to pop music—with one exception: the Beatles. I wondered about that. Sure, the Beatles were geniuses, but what about Elton John? Or Bill Withers? Or Carole King? Why couldn't we play *their* records? I didn't argue, but Phineas, Joey, and I listened to whatever we wanted to anyway. Choir camp turned out cool—until I came down with the flu. So did another boy, David Alba, who was a year younger than me. To avoid infecting the others, we were quarantined together in a dorm room.

At one point, Choirmaster Neslund looked in on us and mentioned that Elvis Presley had just died. Even though Elvis was way before my time, I knew he had impacted the world of music. And I was sorry that he had died so young.

My new roommate, David, was Latino and from Boyle Heights. His dad was a preacher. David was a low-key kid with a sweet nature. We were isolated for three days with nothing to do. We didn't even have a radio. After two days, our health had improved, but to be safe they had us stay a third day. That evening, David asked me a question no one had ever asked before.

Did I know Jesus?

I told David how Grandpa Albert and Mom had taken me to various churches where Jesus was described as a great teacher. David said he understood that, but did I know that he was more than that? Did I know the gospel? No, not really. That's when David began speaking about Jesus and his ministry. David wasn't preachy or pushy. In a plainspoken way, he described a man, the son of God, who lived his life through love. Jesus loved everybody. He accepted everyone. He told everyone to love and to forgive.

David used terms I hadn't thought about before—terms like *salvation*. He said that by accepting Christ's free gift of grace through his sacrifice, we could have everlasting life. All this was said matter-of-factly. David wasn't trying to convince or convert. It was just one kid talking to another. I was interested, even fascinated, but that was it. David didn't ask me to get on my knees and give my life to Christ. He didn't even ask me to pray. He simply spoke from the heart and said what he believed. I had questions he was happy to answer. His explanations made sense, but it was still all new to me.

Then something happened that neither one of us could explain.

In the middle of all this talking, a force entered the room, a weirdly powerful, vibrating energy that shocked us into silence. David looked at me. I looked at him. We were both thinking, *Is this really happening?* It was. The vibrating became even more pronounced. We were trembling, and then we were crying uncontrollably. I wasn't afraid. I was overwhelmed by emotion. I'd never experienced a feeling like this before. After a minute or two, it all stopped.

Inside, I knew what it was. I knew what I'd felt. I'd felt God. I'd felt the living reality of the words David had spoken. I believe that God knew that I needed more than stories to reach me. I needed to be shaken up. I needed an experience that was both spiritual and physical.

In the aftermath, I realized that this epiphany was what I'd been seeking ever since I was a little boy haunted by the trapped-in-the-coffin nightmares. It showed me what Christ had shown the world: that he had conquered death. Believing in his message of all-inclusive love, I had conquered my fear. This epiphany was the remedy. The nightmare never returned.

The next day, David and I were released from quarantine, and we rejoined our choir buddies. I didn't say a thing, but in my heart I knew I had been born again.

Back home, I didn't mention it to Mom or Dad. It was something I wanted to keep to myself for a while. At the same time, I felt a burning need to worship with other believers. Sometime later, a school friend took me to the Berean Seventh-day Adventist church down the hill from our house, on Adams Boulevard, a street lined with African American sanctuaries. SDA's theology combined both sides of me, the New Testament *and* the Old. SDAs obeyed all the Levitical laws, and like Jews they observed the Sabbath on Saturday. The services were spirit-filled: big choir, joyful music. I had mixed feelings about the ceremonial foot washing. It was humbling but bizarre to clean a stranger's toes.

Also bizarre, but in an inspiring way, was the presence of Richard Wayne Penniman, better known as Little Richard, one of the founding fathers of rock 'n' roll. He came to Berean to worship and also preach. I related to him, not just because he called himself a Black Jew, but because I felt his soul in his secular songs. "Tutti Frutti" and "Long Tall Sally" had worldly words but gospel fervor. I could feel the excitement of God in all Richard's music. And I also loved his look: high-coiffed hair, heavy eye makeup, and neon sharkskin suits. Just because I was worshipful in church didn't mean I was moving away from rock 'n' roll.

Beyond the charisma of Little Richard, the real appeal of SDA was the passion of its faith and its clear-cut gospel interpretation. The Bible is an ambiguous book, but as a kid, I didn't want ambiguity. I wanted certainty. And at that time, the SDA interpretation seemed absolute. As a teenager with a new love for God, I wanted instruction.

Mom and Dad were puzzled. They saw me attending a church that, at least to them, was strange. It was also strange for them to see me keeping the Sabbath from sundown Friday to sundown Saturday.

I give Mom credit for giving me space. A spiritual seeker like her father, she realized I was on a journey. And because she was a tolerant person, she wasn't going to get in my way. *Let the boy find God in his own way.* Dad didn't understand. I'm sure he thought I was being ridiculous, yet he kept quiet. He hardly said anything to me anyway, so this was just another topic he could avoid.

Meanwhile, my hyper energy got more hyper. One day, I'd be out smoking dope and digging Black Sabbath with the Dogtown crew, and the next, I'd be singing Fauré's "Requiem" with the California Boys' Choir. Then, on Saturdays, I'd be sitting in church praising the Lord.

And during the week I was a percussionist in the John Adams school orchestra. Meet music teacher Lida Beasley. A tough lady from Texas with a thick drawl, Miss Beasley whipped me right into shape. She was fierce. She had me playing timpani, glockenspiel, marimbas, tubular bells, snare drums, and tambourines. If I fouled up the rhythms, she ran over and played the parts herself. Same for the violinists. The minute they messed up, she'd grab a violin and render the part perfectly. In fact, she could play every instrument, from French horn to clarinet. She was the first musician I had ever seen do that. As time went on, I began to understand what a huge influence the woman had on me. I witnessed the wonder of being a multi-instrumentalist.

Yet at first I couldn't stand her. She was too stern and demanding. She scared us to death. Still, we couldn't deny her skill. We also saw how deeply she cared about excellence. By the end of the first term, I loved her. In turn, she loved us, no matter our musical level. Her passion was great. So was her main lesson: no matter how long it takes, work till you get it right.

In addition to Phineas and Joey, Noah Cotsen was another close choir buddy. He was a good kid whom Mom adored. We were roommates during choir training camp, and we often had sleepovers both at my house and at his home in Beverly Hills. For a kid, Noah was extremely well mannered and sophisticated. He attended the prestigious Harvard-Westlake school in Coldwater Canyon. When his parents sent care packages to camp, they weren't filled with chips and cookies like the rest of us got. Instead, Noah received tins of imported crab, caviar, potted jams, and other worldly delicacies. He was into fashion, skin care, and all the finest things in life. His dad, Lloyd Cotsen, owned Neutrogena soap and collected Japanese art.

Noah turned me on to all kinds of songs. He understood musical nuance. He pointed out, for example, how in Carly Simon's "Nobody Does It Better" the strings' lines respond to the horn punches. Sitting in Noah's room, we must have listened to that record twenty times in a row while Noah jumped up and down on the bed, singing all the different parts, each time growing more excited about the brilliance of the arrangement.

A few days before the next planned sleepover at Noah's, I came home to find Mom waiting for me. I knew by the look on her face that something was terribly wrong. She told me to sit down. She took my hand and, barely able to contain herself, said that Noah, his mother, and another boy from choir named Chris Doering had been murdered in the Cotsens' home. I went numb. I couldn't process it. Things like that just didn't happen to people I knew. I can't remember if I asked Mom how or why it had happened, but even if I had asked, Mom would have had no answers. Answers wouldn't come till later.

All I know was that my friend had been killed. I freaked out. Mr. Cotsen asked me to be a pallbearer at Noah's funeral, but I was too traumatized to attend. I now see that as a weak moment in my life. I wish I could have found the strength, but it wasn't there. I'd never been to a funeral before, and I just couldn't handle it.

When the facts came out, the horror got worse. Mr. Cotsen had sued a Belgian company for producing an imitation of Neutrogena's patented clear amber soap. The Belgian firm lost the suit, and its enraged owner had come to Los Angeles to murder Lloyd Cotsen. But the night he broke into the home, Mr. Cotsen wasn't there. So, the assailant tied up Noah, our friend Chris, and Mrs. Cotsen before shoving them under the dining table. His plan was to confront Mr. Cotsen the minute he arrived home. But when Mr. Cotsen, who happened to be in New York, didn't show up, the Belgian business-man panicked and shot Mrs. Cotsen and the two boys. Mr. Cotsen learned about the murders while he was riding in a cab. Ultimately, the police learned who had committed the crime, but before they could arrest the Belgian in Brussels, the man committed suicide.

At the time of his death, Noah was fourteen.

END OF AN ERA

I was sure that my grandfather would never abandon Bedford-Stuyvesant. Albert Roker loved being a homeowner in a neighborhood where he was seen as the unofficial mayor. He'd been there since the thirties and talked as though he'd be there forever. He walked the streets unafraid. He commanded respect wherever he went. And yet . . .

By the mid-seventies, things had changed. Grandpa had seen crime before. Gangs were a part of Brooklyn life, but gangs had never frightened him. The crack epidemic, however, was something else. It was lethal. Up and down the block, buildings that had once housed families turned into crack dens. Muggings were everyday occurrences. Crack was making people crazy. There were stories about crackheads murdering their own mothers. Anything to get money to buy the drug.

Grandpa was sure the plague would end, but the plague only got worse. Then came the last straw. He was walking his dog, Chubby, through the schoolyard and down Throop Avenue. Grandpa always liked to stop for a couple of minutes and watch the kids play. He was sitting on a bench when Chubby started barking and pulling on his leash. Grandpa didn't understand why the dog was agitated. So, he got up and let Chubby lead him to a corner of the schoolyard where, under a pile of rubbish, Grandpa saw a pair of feet sticking out. He drew closer, pushed aside some of the garbage, and stopped in his tracks. He was staring down on a dead man. Grandpa didn't know if the man had been murdered or had overdosed. All he knew was to call an ambulance and keep the kids away from the corpse.

When he told his daughter the story, Mom said, "Enough's enough." She wanted her parents to move to L.A. She wanted them living close by. They could keep their place in Bed-Stuy, but they needed to get out. Mom then bought them a pretty three-bedroom house in Village Green, a wooded complex just down the hill from Cloverdale.

I was so happy to have my grandparents nearby again. Grandpa provided me with that nourishing fatherly energy I needed. And to have Grandma Bessie within reach was the best. She'd cook my favorite meals, like pancakes and fried chicken wings for breakfast. And I'd get all her beautiful unconditional love. At the same time, I wondered how my grandparents would cope with California. For them both, it was a huge challenge.

After they had been there a couple months, Grandpa had a bout of depression. He didn't know why, but he felt off. This was not in his character. That's when his subconscious took over. He got in his car, drove to the Fox Hills Mall, and walked around for hours, purposely brushing shoulders with people. He realized that was what he needed. He was missing the basic human contact that a sprawling city like Los Angeles, with its isolating car culture, did not provide. He just needed to walk with people to feel whole again.

I'm sure Mom told him about my new spiritual path. I got no questions or pushback from him about my involvement with the Seventh-day Adventists. At the same time, we returned to the ritual we'd started in New York. I went with him to services at the Founder's Church of Religious Science on Wilshire Boulevard. We also went to the City of Angels Church of Religious Science, where the pastor was Reverend O. C. Smith, who'd sung jazz with Count Basie before scoring his pop hit "Little Green Apples." Smith preached that all human hearts are part of an infinite intelligence that we can call God or Spirit or even Christ Consciousness. That was beautiful, but I had begun to think differently. I had accepted Jesus as my personal Lord and Savior.

That message I heard as a kid on Mahalia Jackson records played by Grandma Bessie came full circle. That message had reached my head, but it was now in my heart. I wanted to praise God through the gift that he had given me.

I met some guys at church who really knew how to harmonize. I thought it would be cool if we put together a group. One afternoon, I invited them to my house to work up some hymns. We started with "We're Going to See the King":

"Stepped in the water / Water was cold / Chilled my body / But not my soul / Don't have to worry / Don't have to fret / Come on Jesus/ Jesus, He will fix it!"

And then into, "Hallelujah, hallelujah, we're gonna see the King!"

It was really starting to gel when all of a sudden, my dad came through the front door. He looked us up and down. He was not happy; nor did he even try to be nice.

"What the hell is going on here?"

He reminded me that I wasn't allowed to have anyone over unless he or Mom was home.

"This is different," I said. "This is part of church."

He told my friends to get out. I was embarrassed and humiliated. Dad knew damn well I wasn't doing anything wrong. I mean, here's a kid who isn't having his buddies over to party. We were singing to the Lord! But Dad didn't care. He had to prove that he was the boss.

After everyone left, I went to my room. I waited till Mom got home to complain. She understood, but when it came to marriage, Mom was old school. She reminded me that he was my father, and he had his rules. Mom was devoted to Dad, and Dad was devoted to discipline.

And yet I didn't mind Grandpa's discipline. When he got on my case, he did it firmly but with love. He used to walk up the hill from Village Green and, at 6 a.m., he'd be standing over my bed dripping water on my forehead until I woke up. Time to go to work! And work meant pulling weeds in the backyard, mowing the grass, chopping and bundling wood. I hated it, but I did it. My love and respect for my grandfather overrode my resistance.

And where my father never talked about his past, Grandpa always did. As we worked, doing those chores side by side, he told me stories about his early days in the Bahamas, Miami, and Brooklyn. He never bragged, but he never stopped letting me know that hard work was the only way to succeed. His central message was that you must build a strong foundation. He was adamant about teaching me that achievement doesn't come from luck, but from discipline. Drenched in sweat, he never complained about manual labor. In fact, he reveled in it. He showed me that honest work isn't a burden. It is a joy. And so it is.

MARRIED FOURTEEN YEARS:
AT HOME WITH *THE JEFFERSONS'*
TELEVISION STAR

That was the headline under the color picture of Mom and Dad on the cover of *Jet*, the most popular magazine in Black America. Smiling broadly, Mom was wearing a pink kimono, her hand placed on Dad's shoulder. Dad looked like the happiest man on earth. The caption read, "ROXIE ROKER and her husband Sy Kravitz."

The article said my folks' marriage was "not even typical among Black-White couples. Most of the nations' 421,000 interracial marriages (about 76 percent) involve Black men and White women. But in the minority are such couples as the Kravitzes and Pearl Bailey and Louie Bellson, Leslie Uggams and Grahame Pratt, Chaka Khan and Richard Holland, Maya Angelou and Paul Du Feu, and Minnie Riperton and Dick Rudolph."

In the interview, Dad describes his proposal to Mom: "When I asked her to marry me, she laughed and said, 'You've got to be kidding.' And her mother said, 'He's a nice man, but . . .' And now her mother and I are just the tightest."

Most of the article was about Mom's career, with only one reference to Dad's work. Sy Kravitz, wrote *Jet*, was "venturing into music promotion."

Dad's desire to enter the music world had been building ever since we moved west. With Mom doing so well, he'd been bitten by the showbiz bug. He kept his day job but used his contacts to try to make his own mark. And he saw an opening in pop R&B, where singers like Phyllis Hyman and Angela Bofill were having hits. Soon Dad discovered a good vocalist, Phyliss Bailey, an attractive boom operator on *The Jeffersons*, whom he was sure he could make a star.

Dad had taste. After finding a dozen good tunes, he hired the best sidemen in the city; the best arranger, Barry White's main man, Gene Page; and two great producers, Charlie Colello, who'd worked with Sinatra and Springsteen, and Leslie Drayton, Marvin Gaye's musical director. Dad paid for Phyliss to do a series of showcases at Tom Rolla's Gardenia Restaurant and Lounge, a little club on Santa Monica Boulevard where he cultivated the press. We were there every time Phyliss appeared.

Phyliss got a little press and some good reviews, but her career never took off. Dad was crushed—yet tenacious. His next move was a clothing line. He started one based on fabrics and designs worn by racehorse jockeys. Dad was a gambler, and gambling on a bold concept for men's wear seemed a sure thing. It wasn't. The line went bust.

His next move was to buy a racehorse that never finished first. After that, I lost count of his projects. No matter how many failed, he was always working on a new one, meeting with investors and planning something spectacular. While Mom prospered, Dad's projects stalled. In fact, Mom's earnings paid for Dad's failed ventures.

But man, did he hustle. He was relentless. Like Grandpa, Dad worked every day of his life. He showed me that even when things fail, you keep going. You never stop until you reach your dream. Tragically, I don't think Dad ever reached his.

But there were good times that almost always had a musical soundtrack. Mom and Dad kept up the tradition they'd started in New York, with Bobby Short, of taking me to clubs. We went to the Parisian Room, on Washington and La Brea, to hear Kenny Burrell, the brilliant bop blues guitarist. That's also where we heard Arthur Prysock, a baritone jazz singer who'd sung with Basie. Mom loved her some Arthur Prysock! And then there was a club where we used to go to see Gil Askey and his orchestra. Gil was famous for his arrangements for Diana Ross and the Supremes, the Temptations, and the Four Tops.

My parents and I were regulars at the Playboy Jazz Festival, at the Hollywood Bowl. Our hookup was Mom's close friend Sylvia O'Gilvie, a script assistant to the director of The Jeffersons. Sylvia worked at the festival and scored us a box. It felt like Old Home Week because Bill Cosby, a jazz lover himself, was the permanent emcee. Cosby and Mom were both part of the close-knit community of Black actors working in TV then.

The Playboy Jazz Festival provided an entire day and late into the evening when I could sit next to my dad, not say a word, and enjoy the feeling. He loved the music as much as I did. Playboy was the first venue where I saw Miles Davis live, a major figure in my young adult life. Miles had impeccable style as a musician and a man. He had the courage to break through genres. He broke the mold of the jazz musician and dressed like a rock star. Seeing Miles was always an event.

Then there was the great reunion with his sixties group: Herbie Hancock, Wayne Shorter, Ron Carter, and Tony Williams. I loved how

Miles turned his back to the audience. It was part of his I-don't-give-a-fuck mystique. I also saw it as a way to bring attention to someone he had groomed into a star: drummer Tony Williams, whose hands were moving in six different directions at once.

My folks and I also saw Miles when he was was covering Michael Jackson's "Human Nature" and Cyndi Lauper's "Time after Time." Those songs were a lot tamer than his earlier fusion jams that had such a huge impact on me. That's when Miles threw everything into the mix, including rock guitar and funk grooves. But even the more commercial Miles had charm. Miles never lost his aura. He wore his wraparound shades and his Kohshin Satoh silver suit like a god. He was a bad motherfucker.

My family got close to Miles when he married Godmother Cicely Tyson. We got to hang out. I remember the moment Mom told Miles that I was deep into music. He smiled and nodded silently but approvingly. Over the years, he was always supportive of me. Many said he was detached, but I saw him as an inspiration and an ally. And because Miles didn't bullshit, one encouraging word from him was worth ten thousand words from anyone else.

Miles's validation was fuel. I was eating, living, and breathing music. Mom had bought me a Ludwig natural-finish five-piece drum set that I warmed up by playing to records like George Benson's "Breezin'" and the Jacksons' "Blame It on the Boogie" for hours on end. If Dad wasn't around, I'd have my friends from Crenshaw come up to jam. If Dad was due home, I wouldn't take any chances and I'd go down to their apartments, where I'd play guitar on jams like Earth, Wind & Fire's "Jupiter."

Fooling with all the instruments—drums, guitar, bass, keyboards—I wasn't purposely trying to combine genres; I was just exploring all the different styles I loved. Rock, soul, pop, classical, jazz, funk, whatever. It all felt natural to me.

One day in 1978, Mom was planning a party up at Cloverdale, and I convinced her to let me and my boys perform for her guests. I got together some of the best musicians I knew, and we learned the biggest disco hits. When we started playing, everybody hit the floor. Mom was all smiles, and all her guests were surprised. I'm not sure what Dad thought. He was too busy chatting it up with Max Julien or Roscoe Lee Brown.

A night I'll never forget: I was fast asleep—it was well after midnight—when I was awakened by loud voices coming from the living room. Taj Mahal, the great bluesman, had dropped by after his gig to visit my folks. I had to get out of bed to see him. We all loved Taj's records. We also respected him as someone with an encyclopedic knowledge of world music. Taj is a big man. He has a deep, gruff voice, a no-nonsense manner, and a sweet soul. When I wandered into the living room in my pajamas, wiping the sleep from my eyes, Taj gave me a warm greeting. I mentioned how I'd been playing music. Dad said I should be concentrating more on my school work. "His grades stink, and they're getting worse every year."

Taj looked at me, Taj looked at Dad, and then Taj did something no adult had ever done before. He took on Dad and stood up for my future as a musician.

"I think the kid's doing just fine," he said. "Leave him alone. He knows what he's doing."

That was big. Taj inspired me to redouble my efforts. My excitable energy got more excited. There were bands all over the city I wanted to play with, but how could I get to the clubs? Being up on Cloverdale, far from public transportation, was an obstacle. I had to get down to where the jams were happening. It took me a while to build up the nerve, but I found a way.

One night, I slipped into my parents' bedroom while they were asleep, got on my hands and knees, crawled past their bed, and slowly opened the door to my father's closet. The door made a creaking noise, and I froze. I was scared shitless that Dad would catch me in the act, but he didn't. I was able to get into the closet without waking my parents and reach up to the shelf where he kept the shotgun and car keys. The keys to my mom's car in hand—I didn't dare take my dad's Rolls—I crawled back out, tiptoed to the driveway, put the car in neutral, and rolled it down the hill away from the house before starting the engine and driving off into the night. This was crazy. Friends had just recently taught me to drive. I didn't have a license. I was fourteen years old.

These were artistic adventures, not erotic escapades. In that period, my friendships with girls still fell into the brother-sister category. Girls didn't look at me romantically. They were turned on by jocks or players, and I was neither. I was the nice guy who patiently listened to their problems. When they told me how some asshole had mistreated them, I lent them a sympathetic ear. That was okay with me. I was more interested in chasing down music than girls anyway.

So, those nights, when I stole Mom's Buick, I headed for a jam session or a club. And it was in one of those clubs where I met an amazing green-eyed girl.

A JEWEL

'd just sat in on drums in a club in the San Fernando Valley. I was taking a break when this cocoa-skinned girl with piercing emerald eyes and a seductive smile came up to me. Her face was beautiful. Her body was slamming. Her voice was alluring.

She said she wanted to talk.

Wow. Great.

She asked my age.

I told her and asked hers.

Fourteen.

I was surprised; she looked older.

She said that she was old for her age. She asked if I had a girlfriend.

No.

She thought I was cute. I liked hearing that, but something in her voice sounded off.

Initially, it seemed like she was hitting on me—an exciting first in my life—but then her demeanor changed. After we spoke for fifteen minutes or so, tears filled her eyes and she began to cry. I wanted to know what was wrong. That's when she blurted out the truth: she told me I was a nice guy and she couldn't do this to me.

Do what?

Lie.

Lie about what?

Lie about the fact that she was coming on to me when she really wasn't.

I was confused. I asked her to explain.

She said it was all about my father.

My father?

Yes. Jewel told me she was being controlled by a pimp who had told her to get next to me so she could then get next to my father. Her pimp saw my dad as a potential steady customer for Jewel.

That statement blew my mind. I had no notion of my father dealing with prostitutes. Why would a pimp target Dad? Jewel told me that the pimp knew Dad from the music studio scene.

Jewel had a good soul. I could feel her heart. I could see the purity in her eyes. In spite of the fucked-up assignment she'd been given by her pimp, she had managed to break through the darkness and come out into the light. I saw her for who she was.

Our talk got deeper. She told me that her original abuser had been her dad. She had been passed around at parties to sleep with her father's friends. I was horrified—and also strangely motivated. I had to save her.

I say that not to sound like a hero: heroics were the last thing on my mind. All this was gut reaction. She was as beautiful inside as out. I had to help this girl. I told her that she had to get away from her pimp. But how? She was working out of a seedy motel on Ventura Boulevard in a bad part of the Valley. He kept her under close watch. I told her that no matter how close his watch, she had to get out. *I* had to get her out. Tomorrow.

I formulated a plan. Tomorrow night I'd steal Mom's car again to go get her. She said that was risky. I said that remaining this guy's slave was even riskier. She was afraid of him. I was, too, but something had to be done, and done right away. It had to happen tomorrow night. But what if she had to work? I told her to say she was sick. I'd be there to get her at midnight. I'm not sure she believed me, but she gave me the address of the motel anyway. She was desperate for help.

Next day, I couldn't stop thinking about Jewel. In spite of the power her pimp held over her, she'd been honest with me. Her pimp's scheme to snare Dad pissed me off. I didn't want to think about what it said about my father, so I didn't. I just concentrated on my plan.

The hours dragged by. I turned on the radio. Did I really know what I was doing? Was I ready to tangle with some killer pimp? No. The idea was to avoid the killer pimp. But what if he turned up? Better not think about that. Better just to think about the job at hand. I was resolved and ready.

That night, I did the usual crawl through my folks' bedroom to grab Mom's car keys. My parents didn't stir. I slipped away and drove over to the Valley. I was nervous as hell. If the cops stopped me, I had no driver's license. If Jewel's pimp caught me, I had no gun. Hell, I didn't even have a knife. I also had no real plan except to get Jewel out of the motel.

I got to the Valley and drove down Ventura Boulevard. I reached a block lined with low-rent motels. The one where Jewel said she was staying was lit by a blinking neon sign that cast a scary shade of lurid green over the place. I felt like I was in a horror movie. I parked in front of her room and blinked my headlights on and off. I figured Jewel would be waiting and would run right out. But she didn't.

I got fidgety and was about to get out of the car and knock on her door when a car pulled up next to mine. It was a long-ass maroon sedan. This had to be Jewel's pimp. My heart started racing. I didn't know what to do. I wanted to look over to see who was behind the wheel, but instead I stared straight ahead. I'd find out soon enough.

Whoever was driving the other car turned off the engine. The driver's-side door opened. Then the passenger side. I held my breath. I heard a loud laugh—but it was a woman's laugh. Carefully, I looked up. Right in front of my car stood a tall white woman accompanied by a short white man twice her age. She looked right at me, a big smile on her face. He looked straight ahead. The two of them then strolled a few feet until they reached the room they had reserved. Then they disappeared inside. I thanked God.

Just about then, Jewel opened her door. She waved to me, and I waved back. She went back inside to get her suitcase. I ran out and carried it to the car, still convinced that some motherfucker would come roaring up with a sawed-off shotgun. She told me to hurry because her pimp had only run out to get something to eat and he'd be back any second.

As soon as Jewel was safely in the car, I peeled off like a bank robber. We sailed down Ventura Boulevard, free as birds. For a long while neither of us spoke. Jewel wanted to know where we were going. I wasn't sure. I was still a bundle of nerves. I mean, I didn't even know this girl. I kept driving. She kept thanking me. I kept thinking where I could take her.

I couldn't take her to a friend's house. What would the parents say? No, there was only one place that made any sense—even though it made no sense at all. I had to take her home.

She wanted to know what my parents would say. I said they couldn't know. I'd have to hide her in my room. She had no objections. She was happy because she had escaped from hell.

When we finally drove up to the house, I stopped the car some yards away and turned off the engine. Jewel and I then pushed the Buick into the driveway. We then tiptoed around to the side door that led to my bedroom. Things were even more complicated because, at the time, my cousin Esau's daughter, Jennifer, was living in our guest bedroom while attending college in L.A. Three people to *not wake*.

Once inside my room, I showed her how my bed sat high off the floor. I said there was enough space underneath for a couple of bedspreads and a pillow. She could sleep there. She looked at me funny. Why couldn't she sleep with me?

I said she was beautiful, but this couldn't be about sex. It was about keeping her safe. I had to be the one person she could rely on, the one person she could trust. She had to know that I had no ulterior motive.

It was hard to read her reaction. She looked a little disappointed, but maybe she was just confused. She wasn't used to being treated right.

While she went to my bathroom to change, I slipped into bed. I set my alarm for early enough to get Jewel out of the house before my folks woke up. Exhausted, I fell right to sleep.

Next morning, things went as planned. I showed Jewel how to go out the side door of my bathroom and climb over the fence. She went her way while I went to school. We met back at the house in the afternoon before my folks got back home. I made sure she had enough to eat.

The situation was crazy, but it worked for a whole month. During the day, Jewel would hang out with friends and look for any kind of job. She told me she wanted to turn a page, and I believed her. She said she'd fallen in love with me and offered to do whatever she could to bring me money. That's the last thing I wanted, but I understood that that's how she'd been living her life. I said she had to put all that stuff in the past. We hugged, and sometimes she kissed me on the cheek, but that's as far as it went. I kept my pledge. If I hadn't, I would have hated myself. Hearing her story broke my heart. Like so many lost girls, she'd been taken advantage of by money-hungry men who'd sold her like meat. She just didn't have the strength to fight back.

I knew I couldn't keep this up forever, but at the same time I couldn't find a permanent solution. The routine stayed the same, and the scheme seemed to be working . . . until one fateful afternoon. That's when Jennifer spotted Jewel climbing over the fence to get into our backyard. Jewel knew she'd been seen and ran into my closet. Next thing I knew, Jennifer was in my room, demanding to know what was happening. I told her the truth. Jewel came out of the closet. Jennifer felt compelled to tell Mom. I tried to argue her out of it, but it was no use.

That night was rough. When Mom learned the truth, she flipped out. Fortunately, Dad was out of town. The confrontation started with Mom insisting that I bring Jewel into the living room. She needed to talk to this girl. Jewel was practically shaking. When we got in front of her, my mother had recovered from her initial shock, and now she was calm. It was just the three of us. The first thing Mom asked Jewel was: Where is your family? Where are your people? Jewel told Mom about the situation with her father. I could see that my mother believed her, just as I had. My mother knew how to read people.

Next thing Mom wanted to know was what was going on between the two of us. Jewel said I had been a gentleman. I had placed comforters and pillows under the bed. She swore that we were not lovers, and again, Mom believed her. At the same time, my mother made it clear that this situation could not continue. Something had to be done, and Mom being Mom, she had a solution.

She told Jewel that she and Christina Crawford, the daughter of actress Joan Crawford, were involved with ICAN, the International Council for the Abused and Neglected. Christina had written *Mommie Dearest*, the famous memoir exposing her own abuse at the hands of her movie star mother. My mom explained that, as volunteers, she and Christina had worked with the ICAN faculty. ICAN was a first-rate organization, one where Jewel could receive proper care. Mom then asked Jewel if she was willing to go there. Jewel didn't know what to say. This was a lot to take in. We had just been cold busted by Mom, who was prompting her to go to a facility where she wouldn't know a soul. She looked terrified. Here was my mother—the lady from *The Jeffersons*, of all people!—confronting her. But instead of being hysterical, Mom handled the situation with grace.

Staring at the floor, Jewel took a long time before she responded. No one said a word. Finally, she looked up and quietly said, "I'll go." She was willing to go anywhere she'd be safe. Mom took her hand and said, "Everything's gonna be all right, baby."

That same day, she drove Jewel to ICAN. I came along, but Mom took charge. She helped Jewel through the admissions process and introduced her to her friends on the faculty. Before we left, Jewel and I hugged one last time. She promised to stay in touch.

Jewel was there for several weeks before being released to the care of her grandfather, who ICAN had located in the Crenshaw District. The man was a minister. It all seemed good, but it wasn't.

Not much time passed before Jewel called me to come get her. What was wrong? She couldn't say on the phone, but it was urgent.

When I picked her up, she told me the story. Her grandfather had walked in on her while she was bathing. He said lewd things and made lewd suggestions. In a flash, she saw the same family sickness that had haunted her all her life. She started saying how she was still in love with me and that she would go have sex for money so we could run off together, but I told her to stop. "You can't keep talking like this," I said. In my mind, I knew that this was just her way of expressing love. She sounded so convincing, and she was so fine. But no matter what, we wouldn't be doing that. And I definitely couldn't hide her in my house anymore.

I picked her up and dropped her off at one of her friends' places. She kissed me good-bye, thanked me, and vanished. It would be years before I heard from Jewel again.

THE MOTHERLAND

I was about to enter high school. And because we lived in a predominantly Black neighborhood, I was all set to go to predominantly Black Dorsey High. I liked the idea. I already had friends who went to Dorsey, and besides, unlike my junior high, which was twelve miles away, Dorsey was close by. As it turned out, though, Dorsey was not in my future.

Just as Albert Roker wanted the best education for his daughter, Roxie Roker wanted the same for her son. One day, Mom was talking to Lyle Suter, her classmate from Howard University, who lived down the street on Cloverdale. Lyle ran the art department at Beverly Hills High and convinced Mom that the school's music and arts program was incomparable.

Because we didn't live in Beverly Hills, Mom didn't know how to arrange that. Lyle did. He proposed to the principal that Mom volunteer to teach drama a few times each year. In exchange, they'd let me in. The plan worked, and come September I'd be heading off to Beverly Hills High. But it was only May, and I had a whole summer ahead of me.

I was fine with picking up odd jobs and making music. But leave it to Mom to raise the stakes. How about spending the summer in Africa?

Sure, I'd love to see Africa, but how was she going to pull it off?

Well, Mom had a huge network of friends who adored her. She and Louis Smallwood, for instance, were close as siblings. Louis worked on set as a private tutor for Gary Coleman and Todd Bridges of *Diff'rent Strokes* and Ricky Schroder of *Silver Spoons*. Louis also had lots of side interests, including a partnership with Ben Bruce, a well-to-do Nigerian who owned grocery stores throughout Lagos. Looking to bring African American R&B to Africa, Ben had booked bands into Nigeria's National Arts Theatre for the summer. Louis offered to hire me as the stage manager's assistant. Was I willing?

More than willing, I couldn't wait to jump on a plane.

The preparation, though, turned out to be rough. I'd soon learn that I was super-sensitive to certain meds. The needed vaccinations knocked me out, and the malaria pills didn't work. (More on that in a minute.) But nothing was gonna stop me. I made the flight: LA–New York–Monrovia–Nigeria.

After landing in Lagos, Louis and I were driven to Yaba, a bustling suburb reminiscent of Nassau. I stayed with Ben Bruce's family. They had a good-size home where an armed guard kept watch night and day. That first night almost did me in. It was hot as hell. I slept in a sweltering room on a bed surrounded by mosquito netting. The netting didn't do shit. The mosquitoes ate me alive—for hours. The bites were so severe I became delirious. Ben and Louis had to throw me in the shower to bring back my sanity.

Next day, though sleep-deprived and covered in itchy bumps, I got up determined to hit the streets. First thing I did was expose my naïveté. I asked a police officer where the lions were.

"In the zoo," he said. "Where else would they be?"

I felt like a dumb American kid who had to remember he was in a city with office buildings and businessmen carrying briefcases. The difference, of course, was that everyone was Black. I loved the feeling of being ensconced in an all-Black nation.

Downtown Lagos was cool, but the back streets were even cooler. That's where I made friends. Percussionists banged out beats on all kinds of drums I'd never seen before. I tried every one of them. I spent nights at a dance club housed in a big boat dragged up on dry land. The ultimate discovery that summer was Fela Kuti, the Nigerian musician who had created the social-political genre Afro Beat that had lit up the world. Like Bob Marley, Kuti channeled a universal vibration. He personified African genius. African music was deeply embedded in my soul. Africa spoke to me. Africa *was* me.

I loved Nigeria. I loved the ancient faces of the men, women, and children; the way they walked and ran, talked and laughed; their stark white shirts and dresses; their brilliantly patterned dashikis; their head wraps; their street food—especially *suya*, super-spicy meat on a stick. Dozens of times during the day, I felt so dazed that I had to stop and simply tell myself, *These are my roots.* Like in the Bahamas, I felt extremely connected. I belonged.

On the work side, I got to help out the bands that Ben Bruce had brought from back home, including One Way, featuring Al Hudson, which had dance smashes like "Pop What You Got." These were the days of R&B funk groups like Lakeside and Con Funk Shun.

I liked bringing the musicians sodas and beer. When I couldn't find an opener, a girl my age showed me how to pop open the bottle with my teeth. I couldn't do that, but I could play the drums.

During a tune or two, One Way's drummer let me sit in. African audiences went crazy for the American soul. The gig was great.

I loved Lagos. Still, there were attitudes I didn't understand. I saw so-called upper-class Black employers treat their Black servants sternly, even brutally. That threw me. As an American, I'd seen only whites treat Blacks like this. There was this one guy who had to sit at the front gate of a property in the glaring heat to manually operate the gate to let cars in and out. He would even sleep out there on the ground, to be ready whenever a car pulled up. When I asked the homeowner why he treated him like this, he arrogantly said, "He works for me. That's his job."

I'm sure he felt he had the right, but it really bothered me. Black-on-Black bias repelled me. So did the country's heavy military presence. Crossing from one zone of the city to another, we were always stopped for a full-on search. The soldiers were menacing and short-tempered. Machine guns were shoved in my face. I'd never seen anything like it before. I was frightened, but it wasn't just fear I felt. It was the oppression of a society ruled by brute force.

In spite of that oppression, I was deeply inspired by the motherland and her vibrant children.

On the trip home, Louis Smallwood wanted to stop over in Amsterdam. My first trip to Europe coincided with a mild, yet debilitating, case of malaria. At the Hotel Pulitzer, I was in bed for two days, shivering and sweating and going out of my head. Eventually, the fever broke, my hyper energy returned, and I spent twenty-four hours running around that storybook city, amazed by its old bridges and canals and especially the Bull Dog, a famous hash bar where I was handed a menu of the various strains of weed. A menu! Are you kidding me? A pothead tripping in a city where marijuana's legal? I was stoned ecstatic.

BEVERLY HILLS

As a kid on the Upper East Side in Manhattan, I'd been around luxury and wealth, but Beverly Hills was on another level. I became friends with kids who lived in mansions the size of museums and who were dropped off at school in chauffeur-driven Bentleys. A lot of them drove their own Porsches and BMWs.

One of my first friends was Kennedy Gordy. He was a musician and an all-around good guy who loved to jam. He asked me over to his home in Bel Air. I drove up this winding road that led to a mountaintop overlooking the city. His house felt like a palace. His dad was Berry Gordy, founder of Motown.

On any given day at the Gordys, Diana Ross would be lounging by the pool. Smokey Robinson and Marvin Gaye would be playing cards in the den. The house was heaven! It had everything. One room was a video arcade with all the games I loved. I was used to taking the bus all the way to Westwood to spend my money on these exact same games. And now here they were—all for *free*! Also, you could order any kind of food at any hour from the Gordy kitchen, and someone would deliver it right to Kennedy's room. Oh, and Kennedy's room was filled with all the latest technology: the newest stereos, TVs, and the brand-new Betamax video player. We watched the first full-length porno film I'd ever seen, *Misty Beethoven*. It could not get any better than this.

And then there was the jam room. That was the one filled with sparkling drum sets, guitars, basses, keyboards, and amps. We would play all night, and no one would tell us to stop.

Still another room had a small stage with a piano and mic setup. That's where Mr. Gordy auditioned aspiring artists. Kennedy and I started up our own little group. Once or twice, Mr. Gordy would wander in, listen for a while, smile, say a few encouraging words, and leave.

The Beverly Hills High Music Department really did live up to its reputation, but it took me a minute to adjust. I was just coming off my three-year stint with the prestigious California Boys' Choir, and I was a little snobbed up. I mean, I sang on recordings conducted by Zubin Mehta and performed with the Metropolitan Opera. And now I was a member of a *high school choir*? You could say I had something of an attitude.

Joel Pressman was the music teacher, and I challenged him. But he knew how to handle my arrogance. He, too, had a bit of a personality. Yet he was able to teach me that the music community was all about being gracious and open to new situations. No matter how much you think you know, there's always something more to learn. Mr. Pressman and I were cool.

Same for Mr. Farmer, who taught orchestra, jazz band, and marching band. Confident about my drumming chops, I argued with him about tempo and feel. When he gave instructions, I talked back. I was already playing good guitar, so I wasn't exactly receptive to his critiques. Like Mr. Pressman, though, Mr. Farmer knew how to get to me. He saw I tended to rebel against authority. I'm sure that had to do with my dad. But both teachers saw my potential. They broke down my stubbornness and taught me a lesson I'd never forget: whether you're in a choir, a jazz ensemble, or a marching band, music isn't about confrontation; it's about cooperation.

Beverly High was overrun with talent. One curly-headed dude had the aura of a rock star. His guitar playing was ridiculous. We didn't really know each other well. It was only years later that I became friends with Slash.

Musicals were a big part of the school program. I was a drummer in the orchestra, seated in the pit and playing the score of *Oklahoma*. Onstage, singing the lead role, was Nicolas Coppola, who later changed his last name to "Cage."

I was stimulated by the artistic energy surrounding me in Beverly Hills, but my biggest stimulation was happening two thousand miles away, in Minneapolis. Just as Michael Jackson rocked my world in grade school, Prince rocked my world in high school. When I saw Prince, I saw myself—or at least the me I wanted to be. He could write, sing, dance, and play the shit out of the guitar and every other instrument.

Prince had found a way to funk up New Wave. He knew how to grab attention and create an image. He wore punky clothes and hairdos. He was fearless. In my mind, I heard him saying, *I'm gonna wear a trench coat with nothing but black panties and thigh-high black stockings and ankle boots. I'm gonna wear heavy eye makeup and process the hell outta my hair. I'm gonna do whatever feels good, and you're gonna love it.*

I loved "Soft and Wet," from his first album, and "I Wanna Be Your Lover," from his second. But the release of his third album, *Dirty Mind*, hooked me for life. "Head" was beyond brilliant, not to mention scandalously sexy.

David Bowie was another huge influence. He gave glam swag, and he understood rock as theater. I'd always loved KISS because they were rooted in comic book fun. But Bowie took it further. He kept redefining himself with a mysterious sophistication I recognized as real art. Like Prince, he was cocky and cool at the same time. He had a knack for switching up characters and inventing alter egos like Ziggy Stardust.

I started thinking, *Can I become such a character?*

I kept asking myself, *Who, in fact, am I?*

I started seeing that my search for a look and a voice had been going on since I first saw the Jackson 5. I loved all sorts of voices and all sorts of looks. Now, in high school, I went from an Afro to a short natural to a look-like-Prince process. Ray Hall, Mom's hairdresser on *The Jeffersons*, was the first to relax my hair and fashion it with Jheri curls. I cringe a little when I see photos of myself from back then, but what can I say? That was me, raiding Flip and Aardvark's Odd Ark on Melrose Avenue, sporting vintage tux jackets, ruffled shirts, skinny jeans. This was the New Romantic style. Up on Cloverdale, when no one was home, I'd spend hours in Mom's closet, trying on furs, scarves, and feather hats. Like Prince, I let myself go.

My parents had no idea who I was at night. On my own, I discovered an underground world of music and dancing. The Odyssey was the first place where I felt I belonged—it's where all the misfits gathered. The Odyssey was a cavern that pumped out all the newest

New Wave music, like Soft Cell, Haircut 100, and Romeo Void. Kids wore blousy Elizabethan-style shirts. As soon as I entered, I was hit by the dank smell of butyl nitrite. There was a counter in the back of the club that sold the chemical under the name Locker Room. If I didn't have enough money to buy my own, the stuff was being passed around the dance floor anyway. With my head spinning, I'd dance by myself in the middle of the crowd until 4 or 5 a.m., when I'd have to hurry home to return the stolen vehicle. On other nights, I'd catch a midnight showing of *The Rocky Horror Picture Show* at the Tiffany Theater on Sunset. Stoned and dressed in full costume, I'd dance along to the routines and shout along with the famous dialogue. It was beautiful. It was a fantasy. The whole experience had a communal call-and-response church vibe that brought the freaks together.

Let's do the time warp againnnnnn.

On the home front, things between me and my father had gotten worse. He continued to harp about my bad grades and my messy room. He had a point; he was right on both counts. So, I was always being grounded, but also always finding ways to sneak out anyway. All this was going on while Dad's attempt to make it big in Hollywood was falling flat. His already short temper got shorter.

It was my junior year. I'd just turned sixteen and was leaving the Beverly campus when I spotted this guy blasting Earth, Wind & Fire's "Boogie Wonderland" on a boombox while beating out grooves on a drum pad. He was dressed in a designer suit and fancy Gucci loafers and wearing a gold watch with a mother-of-pearl face and Porsche sunglasses. His hair looked like it had been groomed by

Vidal Sassoon. He was no student. I figured him for a professional musician. Naturally, I had to approach him.

He was a friendly dude: Dan Donnelly. He had just moved back to L.A. from Eugene, Oregon. At eighteen, he'd already graduated high school and figured that by setting up camp on the lawn of Beverly High and blasting out funk, he'd get noticed. His drumming chops were off the charts. When it came to R&B grooves, he was already a virtuoso. His Mexican mother had raised him and his seven siblings by herself.

From that first day on, Dan and I were inseparable. I introduced him to my friends. I talked my music teacher into letting him sit in with the school bands. I acted like his agent. We were both eager to form bands and get our music out to the world. The hustle was on. Dan had me drive his butterscotch-colored Olds Omega so he could beat out grooves on the dashboard until that damn thing was destroyed.

Dan and I soon started up a business based on a model he had developed: a disco/deejay company catering to private parties. Dan supplied the sound system—four Yamaha PA towers—and I learned to deejay. I was up to date with disco and knew which records to buy. I also knew the party scene in Crenshaw, Ladera Heights, and Inglewood. I wasn't shy about soliciting business. We called ourselves GQ Productions, after the men's fashion magazine, and printed up fancy business cards.

The gigs came. We booked everything from sweet sixteens to house parties to cotillions in the ballrooms of fancy hotels. If we were driven to begin with, now we were doubly driven. We were making connections left and right. One of those connections seemed a sure bet.

He was a shady character called Smokey. He claimed that he played drums for the Gap Band. The Gap Band was huge and one of my favorite groups. One night, Smokey heard us jamming—Dan on drums, me on guitar—and he flipped out and said we were gonna be stars. And he was gonna help us form a band. We'd be the leaders, he'd find us sidemen, and we'd soon be touring the world.

Smokey even came up to Cloverdale to meet Mom. My mother skeptically listened to his hype but didn't say a word. When he left, she expressed her doubt. This prompted me to challenge Smokey during our next meeting. I asked him to demonstrate his drumming chops, but he declined. He said he didn't want to show up Dan. Dan and I insisted. That's when we learned that Smokey couldn't play a lick. Not only was he *not* the drummer for the Gap Band, but it turned out he was on crack! Dan and I had been blinded by our ambition. But Mom's eyes were wide open.

That misstep didn't stop me. Nothing would. I kept looking for the right sound, the right voice. I kept looking for my musical self. And this took the form of putting together new bands with new friends.

I was introduced to a guy at Beverly named Tracy Oberstone. He looked so androgynous that most people thought he was a girl. We clicked immediately. Tracy had a Black Jamaican mom and a white Jewish absentee father who hadn't shown up until Tracy was in high school. His dad turned out to be Sy Marsh, a high-powered agent who represented Sammy Davis Jr. When Marsh finally did appear in Tracy's life, it was only to drop off a bag of second-hand clothes. I was a witness to that sad scene. To complicate things even more, Tracy learned that one of our high school friends, Tracy Marsh, was Sy's daughter! His dad had never even bothered telling him that he went to school with his half sister, not to mention that she shared his name!

Reed thin with a headful of ringlets, the male Tracy had a vibe that, in the Prince/Michael Jackson days of the early 1980s, I was sure was right for a band. And as one of the boy dancers on *The Tim Conway Show*, he was already a pro. Tracy's gender-bending Mick Jagger silhouette gave him the look of a lead singer. In fact, the first thing I asked him when we met was "Can you sing?" He said, "Not really," but that didn't stop me. I took him to my house and, playing piano, began training him.

Tracy and I scraped together enough money to book a little studio on Western Avenue and cut a song we'd just written, "Love Me Up." Dan was on drums, I played all the other instruments, and Tracy sang lead. Using the Beverly Hills High/Hollywood connection, we gave the tape to our classmate Jill Bogart, to give to her dad, Neil, who owned Casablanca Records, home to Donna Summer and KISS. Bogart called the song "encouraging" and said he wanted to hear more. But no contract followed. At age sixteen, I was already looking for a major record deal.

Because Tracy's mom was so chill, I liked hanging at his house at 310 North La Peer, in the Flats, a middle-class section of Beverly Hills, where they rented the upper floor of a duplex. His big brother, Mark, had a Marantz stereo system, cable TV, and, best of all, an oversize bong. *Playboy* Playmate posters covered the walls. This was the room where I first got blasted on Michael Jackson's *Thriller*.

Because of my dad's uptight vibe, my house was far less friendly than Dan's or Tracy's. Dan could handle my folks—he and Dad bonded over jazz—but Tracy couldn't. When I introduced him to her, his first words were "Hey, how you doin', Rox?"

My mouth hit the floor. For all her easygoing charm, my mother was dignified. She comported herself correctly at all times. Etiquette was paramount. A child did not address a grown woman by her first name unless given permission to do so. My other friends knew to call her "Mrs. Kravitz." In this instance, though, not wanting to cause a stir, Mom gave Tracy a pass. She simply smiled hello, but I knew she was thinking, *Who does this kid think he is?*

When similar incidents occurred, Mom continued overlooking Tracy's lack of decorum. But then came the reckoning. It happened because Tracy was over after Dad had forbidden me to have company. Mom graciously offered to drive him home. On the way to his house, Tracy started lecturing my mother on how she and Dad were raising me wrong. He argued that the discipline in the Kravitz household was too strict and that I needed more freedom. Mom just kept driving. She didn't say a word. And Tracy kept going on about the deficiencies in her parenting. Finally, Mom had had enough. With her left hand on the wheel, she took her right hand and slapped Tracy across the face. Hard. That shut him up.

When they arrived at Tracy's house, she took him to the door and asked to speak to his mother.

"I slapped your son," she said. "And I want you to hear it from me so you'll know exactly why."

Mother to mother, she explained what had happened. She had struck Tracy, she said, because he was being disrespectful. She hoped Tracy's mom would understand. Tracy's mom did understand. From that day on, Tracy called Mom "Mrs. Kravitz."

TOO FAST

Mom didn't like my first serious girlfriend, Penelope. A couple of years younger than me, Penelope wore super-short miniskirts, drank, smoked, and snorted coke. And she was the first person with whom I started exploring sex. Mom described her in two words: *Too fast*.

"That girl's got more lines on her face than I do," she said.

She thought I could do better. I didn't see it that way. Penelope loved sex and had a lot of experience. Truth is, given what my friends were doing, I was late to the game. But that was okay. I wasn't in a hurry. I wasn't interested in convincing or coercing women. That's because I'd been coerced myself and didn't like it.

It happened when Mom and Dad went away for a week's vacation. Not wanting to leave me unsupervised, Mom invited her friend Nigel, a charismatic actor of West Indian descent, to stay at the house and watch me. Inadvertently, she'd put the fox in the chicken coop! Nigel was a swinging bachelor in his late forties. He dug beautiful women in their early twenties, and he threw pool parties where the two could come together. Difficult as it was, I tried to keep my cool around the bikini-clad women hanging out in my parents' backyard.

One night, I was in my room sound asleep when I felt someone slipping into bed with me. I opened my eyes and saw it was one of Nigel's chicks—topless. When she started taking off my pajamas and going down on me, I stopped her. I told her I had a girlfriend.

She said it didn't matter.

I said it did.

She got angry. She asked, "You're not attracted to me?"

I said I was, but that wasn't the point.

What was the point?

I didn't want to cheat on my girlfriend.

That was true, but also, if I didn't have to pursue a lover, I wasn't turned on. I loved the ritual of seduction. I loved the chase: the conversation, the mental stimulation, the buildup, the candlelight, the music. I didn't want it just laid at my feet.

She was persistent. But I was even more persistent. Nicely, I told her to leave.

When Mom and Dad returned from their vacation, they asked me how the week had gone. Of course, I wasn't going to bust Nigel and shatter Mom's illusions about her good friend. I just said that everything had gone well.

Penelope and I didn't last long. Even if a relationship turned romantic, it seemed I had to establish a genuine friendship first.

That's what happened with Cynthia, a friend from Beverly High who lived in Windsor Hills, a Black neighborhood close to Cloverdale. When I was in the marching band, Cynthia was a cheerleader. There was strong solidarity among the Black kids at school—we all sat together in the cafeteria—but Cynthia, like me, was part of every social group. At one point, she dated the white quarterback, which tripped out the white girls. She had a free spirit and a bubbly personality. Everyone loved her, especially Mom. Because my mother understood our relationship, Cynthia was the only one of my female friends allowed to spend the night. If she and I were up late watching taped episodes of *Saturday Night Live* with Eddie Murphy and she fell asleep on the couch, Mom would welcome her to stay over—that is, she could remain on the couch, not in my bedroom. Cynthia was also ahead of her time. During an era when girls weren't likely to ask boys out on dates, she didn't mind doing so in the least. She also had a strong spiritual side.

Cynthia soon became a permanent part of our household. Every time I turned around, she was there. She even thought that Sy Kravitz was fly. Cynthia had a far better relationship with my father than I did. But that's not saying much: everyone got along better with Dad than me. The heat between us had been boiling since day one. Now it was about to boil over.

BEVERLY HILLS AND BOHEMIA

THE BLOWUP

The thunderous clash with my dad came in the spring of 1981. I was sixteen. It happened the night that Dan Donnelly and I were set to drive down to Anaheim to catch the legendary Buddy Rich and his big band at Disneyland. As a drummer, I aspired to emulate Buddy's immaculate single-stroke roll.

To make a statement, Dan and I dressed up in suits and ties. Just as we were leaving the house, Dad stopped me.

You're not going anywhere.

Why?

You were out last night.

What does that have to do with tonight?

If I've told you once, I've told you a hundred times. You can't go out with your room looking the way it does.

I said I'd clean it up later.

He said he didn't care. I was grounded.

Not tonight, I said. Buddy Rich is playing. You know he's great.

Dad knew, but at this moment, he didn't care. He was adamant. I wasn't to leave the house.

But we have tickets.

Let Dan go and give the other ticket away.

That's *my* ticket. I'm going.

The hell you are.

The hell I'm not.

It escalated from there. Dad got in my face, but for whatever reason, that didn't scare me. I wasn't budging. Neither was he. And then something snapped. I put up my fists. I said I was tired of his shit. I said I'd kick his fuckin' ass. The truth is that he could have wiped me out in a second. I was no match for the man. But my stance shocked him. Looking back, I know he wasn't afraid of me; he was probably more afraid of how he would destroy me. So, instead of getting physical, he kept it verbal. He said if I left now, I'd be leaving for good.

Fine. I'd leave for good.

I threw a bunch of my stuff in a duffel bag and moved out of the house. And that was it. I'd never live in Sy Kravitz's house again.

At the time I had no plan B. I had no plan whatsoever. I didn't know where or how I'd live. But that didn't matter. Despite the pain it would bring Mom, I knew I had to get out. I wasn't afraid. I was resolved.

First things first, though. Let's go down to Disneyland to catch Buddy!

That night, the drummer was on fire. His band was burning. The music was so intense that I forgot all my problems. Once the show was over, though, my mind went back over what had transpired earlier that evening.

The confrontation with Dad shook me up but didn't break

me down. I knew I could survive. I had friends who would let me crash in their homes. I could couch-surf. And meanwhile I had plans to make music. GQ, our disco party outfit, was growing.

My only worry was Mom. She had always tried to make it right between me and Dad. My leaving would break her heart. At the same time, I couldn't stay for her sake. I had to take my life into my own hands.

That first night, I crashed at Dan's. Next morning, I moved in with Tracy Oberstone. First thing I did was call Mom. Naturally, Dad had told her about the confrontation. I said I was fine and staying at Tracy's. Mom insisted on talking to Tracy's mother, who reassured my mother that I was welcome there. Then Mom got back on the line with me.

She said I needed to cool down. I agreed. She thought my move was temporary. I knew it was permanent, but I didn't need to tell her that. I didn't need to add to her aggravation. She made me promise I wouldn't quit school, a promise I kept. She had every expectation that I'd go on to college. But I knew I'd be lucky to graduate high school.

I loved staying at Tracy's. He became like a brother to me. We have the same sense of humor and could finish each other's sentences. His mom, Dorsay Dujon, was cool, and his brother, Mark, was funny. Compared to my father's boot camp, the Oberstone household was paradise. Dorsay was gone all day, so we could do whatever we wanted: listen to music, make music, skip school. Mark had the best weed, the best bong, and a serious stereo system. The mini fridge in Tracy's bedroom was stacked with beers. We stayed up as late as we liked.

There was, though, a negative side. I quickly learned that for

Black people, life in Beverly Hills, one of the richest enclaves in America, could be treacherous. This hit home for me when Tracy, Mark, and I pulled into a gas station. Out of nowhere, three squad cars came roaring in and surrounded us. Guns drawn, they ordered us out of the car and forced us facedown on the ground.

Then, just as they were ready to get rough, up popped Mrs. Freeman, my history teacher, a kind woman who'd always let me leave class to play music. She stood up to the cops, demanding to know what was going on. The police said a car matching ours had been used in a robbery, but when Mrs. Freeman insisted that they double-check their information, they learned that they'd made a mistake. Without Mrs. Freeman intervening that night, we could have wound up in jail—or worse.

Instead, we went back to Tracy's duplex and dealt with the incident by treating ourselves to a lavish homemade dinner. We barbecued steaks with tater tots. I cooked my specialty, shrimp scampi. To add to our sense of sophistication, we pooled our money and bought a few bottles of Royal, an imported Holland brew that came in an opaque designer bottle. Buzzed on beer, we put the police drama behind us.

While I was living with Tracy, he had an audition for a stage revival of *The Me Nobody Knows*. The director was George Wolfe, who'd later gain fame for *Jelly's Last Jam* and *Angels in America*.

Tracy and I went to the theater together. I waited outside while he went in to read. A woman holding a clipboard asked if I was there to audition. I said no. She told me she worked for the casting agent and wanted to know if I could act and sing.

Well, yes.

She liked my look and urged me to try out.

I figured I had nothing to lose. And I figured right. I got the part, and Tracy didn't. I was worried he would be upset, but being a seasoned pro he was cool.

The Me Nobody Knows had originally opened in 1970 in New York, featuring twelve inner-city kids (eight Black and four white), each of whom sang a song. Each tune defined his or her character. It was an interesting dramatic vehicle and good enough to win an Obie. Tisha Campbell was in the cast of our revival. Tisha had these hazel eyes I couldn't stop staring at. She also had the most beautiful singing voice and the sweetest personality. A working professional since she was a little kid, Tisha had been one of the stars in the original Broadway production of this very play. She was a Jersey girl from East Orange, and her street smarts and swagger gave her an attitude I found sexy. I suppose I caught her eye, too, and we started flirting. Next thing I knew, we were making out on the floor during a party at a cast member's place in Hollywood.

George put on a number of scaled-down productions for backers, but the backers didn't bite, and the revival never ran. The run was over, and Tisha had to go back home to New Jersey. We were in love, and I told her I'd come see her as soon as I could. I kept my promise.

Another obstacle to my newfound freedom: my GQ party opera-tion with Dan had long ago run out of steam. The gigs had stopped. That meant finding any kind of job I could get.

Louis Smallwood, the friend of Mom's who'd brought me to Africa, had just bought a "you buy, we fry" fish joint called Leroy's, located on Washington Boulevard and Rimpau, where locals bought their red snapper, turbot, catfish, sand dab, and flounder. Louis hired me as a counterman. I seasoned the orders with corn-meal and pepper, fried 'em up, and threw 'em in a basket with a side of potato salad, macaroni salad, and two slices of white bread. Don't forget the ketchup and hot sauce.

Catfish was especially nasty to prepare. I had to cut open the fresh fish and remove its reproductive system, a whole apparatus of chambers and ducts and eggs covered in blood. Then I diligently scraped the fish till it was clean. Tom Bradley, L.A.'s first and only Black mayor, never failed to show up at Leroy's for his Friday night fish fix before being driven off to his Hancock Park mansion.

I loved Leroy's. Great characters populated the place—hustlers and funny old dudes straight outta Richard Pryor routines, like Redbone, a Jheri-curled Creole brother who couldn't stop talking about his talent for eating pussy.

Because I was gutting, cutting, and frying fish, I stank to the heavens. Standing over the fryer for hours at a time also caused major pimple breakouts from the oil and grease hitting my face. After work, if Dad wasn't home, I'd go up to Cloverdale to visit Mom. The first thing she did was make me take a shower with lemons, the only way to get rid of the smell of fish.

By then, I'd moved out of Tracy's and was living in a Pinto I rented for $4.99 a day. I slept in the reclining front seat, but it was better than sleeping in the park. I also found a second job, as a dishwasher at East West Café, on Melrose Avenue, across from Fairfax High. Mom would come there for lunch, just to make sure I was okay and still in school. I was, but I wasn't about to tell her I was living in a car. The East West gig had its upside: the kitchen window looked out onto an alleyway where my friends would come to keep me company while I scrubbed pots and pans.

The less gritty jobs were actually tougher on me. My stint at GHQ (Gentlemen's Headquarters), at the Beverly Center mall in West Hollywood, was a bust. I wasn't good at sales, and I didn't like pushing high-priced clothes I wasn't into myself. I'd rather have fried fish or washed dishes than tell someone he looked good in a silk suit when, in fact, he didn't.

So I lived out of that car. I lived on the fly. I was a strange combination of high school kid and hustling musician. And for a while an amazing artistic family, the Steinbergs, took me in. That opened still another world to me.

I'd become friends with Eliza Steinberg in my second year at Beverly, during school orientation. She was a year younger, and I was performing with the school band to inspire freshmen to join the arts programs. There was an immediate attraction and instantaneous bonding. I had two very different kinds of feelings for girls I found attractive. I saw them either as girlfriends or sisters. It's no surprise that the sister relationships were the ones that lasted longest. It wasn't that there wasn't love between me and Eliza—there was deep love—but the kind of enduring love you feel for family.

Eliza's family embraced me. Their Angelo Drive house off Benedict Canyon was a work of minimalist art, starting with the gray industrial carpet. Eliza's mother, Lenny, was a gifted decorator and artist who designed her own furniture. Her husband, Bob, was a lawyer. The three Steinberg sisters were dancers, choreographers, and filmmakers: Eliza's sister Morleigh created a body of work all her own (and wound up marrying The Edge, of U2), and Roxanne conceived a series of pieces with her Japanese husband, Oguri, master of the Butoh school of dance. Eliza was herself a great dancer and loved learning the latest moves from the Black girls at school. She and I would go to parties together in Baldwin Hills and Inglewood and dance the night away.

It was Lenny Steinberg who introduced me to Maxfield, a West Hollywood boutique where I first saw the work of Issey Miyake and

Yohji Yamamoto and learned that clothes (like paintings or dance or music) have no creative limits. Already a clotheshorse, I now saw the relationship between high fashion and art.

The Steinbergs became my refuge. Or, as Eliza's dad said, his daughter brought me home, and I never left. When my cousin Jennifer got married in Nassau, I took Eliza as my date. By then, she was my sister.

It was the Steinbergs who helped me heal my rift at Cloverdale by becoming friends with Mom and Dad. Knowing the friction between me and my father, Lenny and Bob invited my parents and grandparents to their home. It was an especially gracious move. Mom and Lenny Steinberg got along famously, and so did Grandpa Albert and Bob Steinberg. The two bonded over baseball and philosophy. Later, Mom reciprocated by inviting the Steinbergs to Cloverdale. That evening also went great. These social occasions allowed my parents to see that, while I was still living outside their home, good people were looking after me.

Eliza Steinberg and Tracy Oberstone were both in Miss Janet Roston's famous dance class at Beverly Hills High, where the artistic standards were incredibly exacting. A third member of that class, Jane Greenberg, became my sweetheart and lifelong friend. Like Eliza, Jane had great artistic spirit, a sweet nature, and an appreciation for what I was trying to do musically. The first time I saw her in her Fred Segal skinny jeans and a cashmere sweater, I fell in love. When we got to talking, the chemistry was strong. We both craved emotional intimacy. Jane wasn't an attention seeker; she was a spiritual seeker, someone I could talk to all night long. The obstacle we faced wasn't our feelings for each other, but Jane's parents.

Jane's folks were liberal Jews. Her dad was an attorney who'd helped launch the LA Opera. Her mom was a member of the board of the Museum of Contemporary Art. Their Beverly Hills home was filled with paintings by Roy Lichtenstein and Franz Kline. Jane's grandparents had an even more expansive art collection, Picassos and Pollocks. Yet, for all their passionate commitment to the arts, it didn't feel like Jane's parents wanted their daughter dating a Black boy.

Sometimes, after working at Leroy's, I'd park the Pinto down the street from the Greenberg home and sleep in the backseat, hoping the cops wouldn't come banging on the window. I'd wait till morning, when Jane's folks would leave for the day. Then Jane would let me in to shower. The Greenbergs' housekeeper, Frances, was like an auntie and always made sure I had something to eat.

Jane and I hung out at the Beverly Hills Public Library, poring over books on art and sculpture. That's how she got in trouble. One day, while we were walking back from the library holding hands, someone saw us and snitched to Jane's parents. More fireworks. This stalled us but didn't stop us. I kept slipping Jane little love notes. We kept meeting on the sly at the Bagel Nosh, where we fantasized about our future: she saw me as a jazz musician living in New York. I saw her by my side, writing poetry and the great American novel on an old Underwood typewriter.

Our amorous adventures continued. During the summer, I drove out to visit Jane at the Idyllwild Arts Academy, in the San Jacinto Mountains, where Bella Lewitsky, the modern dance innovator, led the faculty. The Steinberg sisters were there, too, along with another friend, Julie, daughter of actors Martin Landau and Barbara Bain.

Jane and I spent the night together in her dorm room. Heaven.

Then hell: on another trip, I somehow got Dad to let me borrow his car and totaled it head-on into a tree. I'd been sober but reckless: I was driving too fast on a winding road late at night. I thought Dad would never recover, but this time he was surprisingly understanding. He paid for the towing and didn't give me shit for destroying his car. He was just grateful I was alive.

Jane understood me and pushed my sense of fashion. Long before Jean-Paul Gaultier, she custom-designed a man's skirt made of jersey. I decided to wear it on a night that she and I were going dancing with Phineas Newborn and Joey Collins. Before the evening began, we were all up at Cloverdale. Dad was still at the office, so the coast was clear.

When I came out wearing a black-on-black shirt with a subtle floral print, a black tux jacket, and . . . the black jersey skirt, Phineas and Joey whistled their approval. Jane beamed with pride. Mom stayed silent. Keep in mind, Mom adored Phineas, Joey, and Jane. Still, she was facing her son in a skirt. After my friends' applause died down, my mother continued staring at me. Straight face. Finally, she spoke:

"If you're gonna wear that skirt, you need to change your shoes. Those shoes are not working."

Okay. Most of the guys I was hanging out with then were gay. And although she never asked, Mom had to have been wondering which way I was going. Most moms would not have let their son leave the house in a skirt. But Roxie Roker wasn't most moms. Scrutinizing me up and down, she just needed the outfit to work. It was like, *Baby, you gotta coordinate.*

How cool is that?

WAVE

Jane went off to boarding school in Switzerland, but our bond never weakened. When she learned that I was dead broke and couldn't afford an amp for one of the endless bands I was putting together, she bought one for me. And even though she wasn't living at home, I went by the Greenberg house just to give Frances the housekeeper a hug.

During those first years after I left home, I found shelter with friends like Dalee Henderson, Mom's beloved hairdresser, who worked at Tovar, a Beverly Hills salon. Dalee was an elegant Black southern gentleman, regal in bearing and super sharp. He had an infallible eye for everything from clothes to furniture. I saw him as a true trendsetter, fearless and fierce in his style.

These were the days of heavy chemicals: extreme straightening and outlandish coloring. Dalee was a master alchemist; his coifs were high art. He took me to the hottest clubs in West Hollywood: Studio One; Rage; Peanuts, a lesbian bar; and Jewel's Catch One, on Pico, one of the first Black gay dance bars in the city. Dalee supported my wanderlust lifestyle by housing me when I had nowhere to sleep and feeding me when I had nothing to eat, as well as by keeping my hair fresh. As my look evolved, he chided me for picking the wrong shirt and praised me for wearing the right boots. Dalee knew Mom so well that when I was wearing one of her necklaces, he recognized it immediately. He was a loving big brother.

Half of Mom's friends were gay. The only difference between them and me was that I wasn't sexually attracted to men. Otherwise, I had more in common with them than I did with most straight guys. Fashion, music, photography, design—you name it, gay men helped me form my sense of style. They were the trailblazers, the ones creating the avant-garde culture in L.A.

Meanwhile, at Beverly Hills High, I cared about only one thing: the music programs. I never stopped working on my chops. But it got to the point where no matter how well I was doing in music, I was still in danger of flunking out. I didn't care. I was focused on forming some kind of group to score a deal. I was still searching for my voice. That search would go on for years, but that didn't stop me from wanting to record. Inside, I knew what I had to do. I had to make music.

I had promised my mother that I wouldn't drop out of school. But despite that promise, I was on the verge of doing so—until Mom, as always, came to the rescue. She had learned about Newbridge, a private school specializing in problem kids. Many of its pupils were the children of celebrities who'd washed out of other schools and required extra attention.

The vibe at Newbridge was hippy-dippy. We called our teachers by their first names. There was no real discipline. In fact, a big sign hanging in the hallway read, "Question Authority." Some of the students and teachers even smoked weed together. In one case, a teacher was actually dating a student.

I liked the loose attitude, but I still didn't study. My mind was fixated on music to such a degree that I snuck over to Beverly Hills High and, thanks to the kindness of Mr. Farmer, continued jamming with the jazz band.

It was jazz that kept my relationship with Dad from falling apart completely. Even after I left home, the Playboy Jazz Festival remained our yearly ritual. That first time after I'd left home, we sat together, appreciating Freddie Hubbard and Chick Corea and Al Jarreau. In unison, we tapped our feet to the Toshiko Akiyoshi–Lew Tabackin Big Band. Mom and Dad held hands during Nancy Wilson's set. Because my mother was friends with Sarah Vaughan, she took me backstage before the show. Sarah was in her dressing room wearing a plain muumuu. Barefoot, she was drinking, smoking, and snacking on chips. "Child, come give me a hug." Sarah was the salt of the earth. She and Mom chatted it up, while I watched in awe.

Fifteen minutes later, I was seated in our box, sandwiched between Mom and Dad. Lights down. Pin spot on Sarah as she entered wearing a long gown glittering with silver sparkles. Her command of the stage was stunning. Her voice—her rich tone, remarkable range, ability to bend notes with striking beauty—wiped me out. Five minutes before, she'd been Auntie Sarah. Now she was a regal queen.

How do you go from falling head over heels in love with the voice of Sarah Vaughan to organizing a New Wave band? I didn't think twice about it. Music inspires me, pure and simple. Inspiration comes from all genres. The same way I was a couch surfer, I was a genre surfer. Riding the waves of new music.

My biggest operation so far was a band named Wave. It was the Gap Band meets the Jacksons meets Rick James meets Shalamar meets the Time—with solid chunks of heavy rock thrown in for good measure. Four horns, two keyboardists, a bassist, Dan on drums, two guitarists, and a girl backup trio I named Wet.

Tracy took the lead. His rock star aura made him a perfect front man.

The second singer was Kevin Conner, my boy from Bed-Stuy. Kevin and I had been tight since we met as little kids. During my time in California, he'd been making strides as an amateur boxer in Brooklyn, but I convinced him to sing. Kevin was a serious music fan. He knew every Marvin Gaye riff, and I knew he'd fit in fine. I scrounged up the money, sent him a plane ticket, and, in another one of my crazy schemes, snuck him into Cloverdale. I may not have been living there anymore, but for months Kevin camped out in a sleeping bag in the alcove outside my bathroom door. When Mom and Dad went out for the day, I'd bring him sandwiches from Leroy's, where I was still frying fish.

All went smoothly until Dad heard a noise, grabbed his shotgun, and nearly blew Kevin away before realizing the "intruder" was Kevin from Bed-Stuy. Mom would have let him stay, but not Dad. So, I found Kevin another place to crash. I also had Dalee do his hair and dress him in a pink polo shirt, designer jeans, and K-Swiss sneakers. The Beverly Hills girls went crazy for him, and Kevin hooked up with a sweetheart who lived in a mansion bigger than Berry Gordy's.

I was Wave's third singer. I wasn't looking to be the star— that's never been my goal—but rather, the guy who makes it all happen—a junior Maurice White. Wave was never a cover band.

We wrote original songs. With Earth, Wind & Fire in mind, I also hooked up fog machines, sound effects, and an elaborate light show. And Tracy, Kevin, and I made our own costumes. We went to a fabric store in West Hollywood and bought cheap vibrant prints and fake leather to make trousers. Then we hit up Flip for vintage shirts, which we bedazzled with rhinestones. We finished off the look with Prince-like pompadours, Michael Jackson Jheri curls, and smoky eye makeup.

We'd rehearse at Martin Landau and Barbara Bain's house. They didn't seem to care that their basement was overrun with kids blasting funky music. Within a matter of months, we'd put together a fifteen-member band on a shoestring.

The idea was to introduce Wave at a heavily promoted show where, before storming the stage like rock stars, we'd arrive in limos. But naturally, limos cost money. Because I was not only writing songs and putting together this major production, but had assumed the role of super salesman, too, I convinced my Newbridge classmate Michael O'Connor, who came from a wealthy family, to underwrite the show. I also talked the Music Department at Beverly Hills High into letting us use the school's auditorium. I was a man possessed. This show had to happen, and it had to be nothing less than spectacular.

To hype the event, we did an interview for the local paper and printed out embossed tickets:

Fantasy Productions Proudly Presents
WAVE
In Concert: Friday, December 3, 1982, 8 PM
Beverly Hills High, K.L. Peters Auditorium
421 South Moreno Drive, Beverly Hills, California
FREE ADMISSION

The big night arrived. Naturally, Mom came, but I was glad that Dad did, too. After all this work, I wanted my father to see what I was about to pull off. And we did pull it off. The kids went nuts. No one expected anything this extravagant: the professional sound system, the lighting, the wardrobe, the eleven-piece band.

The response to our original music was immediate. We crushed it. During a slow baby-making bedroom ballad, I fell to my knees. The girls in the front row reached out to touch my hands, and I reached back to touch them. They screamed. Straight out of the Teddy Pendergrass handbook.

As the last song ended, we looked out and, through the foggy lights, saw the entire crowd on their feet, cheering. We did it.

After the show, backstage was crazy. People who had never even cared to talk to me were trying to get at me. It was like the backstage scenes I'd experienced growing up. Amid the chaos, Mom and Dad found me.

Mom was knocked out.

Dad was not. His words stopped me cold: "There's only one person with talent up there, and that's you."

In one weird sentence, he'd delivered both an insult and a compliment. I didn't know what to say.

Later, the band and our entourage piled into the limos we'd rented and drove over to the after party. And that's where I fucked up.

I'd been dating Terri, a stunning Japanese American girl who was in our backup group, Wet. Terri lived in an old Craftsman house in Santa Monica. She and I were really close. She cared about me. But I hadn't finished things with Penelope, my first love. Terri was a big believer in my talent. Penelope was not; she'd even written me a letter saying I'd never make it as a musician. And that's why I invited her to see the Wave show. I wanted to prove her wrong.

So, feeling vindicated, I showed up to the after party with Penelope. Terri was heartbroken. She had every right to be. I acted like a jerk.

That wouldn't be the last time. A girl I knew from Beverly didn't have a prom date and asked me to go with her. I didn't really want to go, but the Roxie Roker people-pleasing part of me accepted. Then, the day before the big night, I called her and said I couldn't go. I backed down because I wasn't attracted to her; I was also worried about what other people would think. I felt bad, but I was immature then. My insecurities overrode the commitment I'd made to her. This was not how my mother had raised me. I wasn't proud of that moment. Another asshole move.

My relationships with both Penelope and Terri fizzled out. Yet, in the aftermath of the Wave show, things shifted. Girls came looking for me. The old sister-brother paradigm faded fast. When my folks were out for the evening, I'd sneak girls up to Cloverdale to party. That house was a great backdrop for my rendezvous, a sexy interior, the Isley Brothers on the turntable, the glow of the pool, the lights of Los Angeles sparkling like diamonds in the distance.

I graduated Newbridge by the skin of my teeth. But I honored my pledge to Mom. I made it out of high school. I had a college fund set aside for me, but obviously I wasn't about to enroll. My focus was on getting a record deal. Even though Dad had said he had more faith in me than in the band, I couldn't see myself ditching Wave. I'd put so much into the group. At the same time, maintaining the band cost a fortune. Wave wasn't practical. *Maybe*, I thought, *Dad'll change his mind and back us*. I invited him over to Tracy's house so we could talk it over.

When Dad arrived, Tracy, Kevin, and I were prepared with a plan to keep the band going. To cut demos, we'd need money for studio time. Dad wasn't impressed. He didn't mince words. With

Tracy and Kevin sitting right there, he said he wouldn't put a cent into Wave. He would, though, allow me to use my college fund to make demos that featured me and me alone.

Kevin wasn't really invested in the group. He was more interested in chasing pussy. But Tracy was seriously offended. Like me, he was committed to Wave. Dad couldn't have cared less about Tracy's feelings, though. But that was Dad; he was all business. He reiterated his core belief: I might be worth it, but the band wasn't.

I had mixed feelings. For the first time in my life, my father was expressing support for me—but at the expense of my friends. These were my brothers.

I thought about defying Dad and saying, "No, it's Wave or nothing." But I knew damn well that approach would get me nowhere. The only way to access my college fund was to work on my own material. In the end, that wasn't a bad option, even if it did mean the end of Wave.

It's ironic that Dad, who opposed me in so many ways, was the first to push me into becoming a solo artist. And that got me thinking in new directions.

I thought a lot about David Bowie. Musical genius aside, he was another fashion icon who spoke to my sense of style. I was intrigued by his contrasting eyes, one brown, the other blue. Bowie was the reason I decided to get color-changing contacts. I thought sky-blue eyes would look cool. Little did I know that the decision, completely cosmetic, would have huge spiritual implications.

SPIRITUAL VISION

In search of blue contact lenses, I was led to an ophthalmologist in Glendale who'd done work for Universal Studios. He'd actually created the special effect contact lenses used by the title character in *The Incredible Hulk*. His name was Dr. Joseph Scimonetti. It was a long ride to his office in the north San Fernando Valley, but the trip was worth it. Dr. Scimonetti, I'd learned, hand-painted the contacts himself. And I could choose any shade of blue.

These were the days before soft lenses. Back then, contacts were thick; they felt like bottle caps in my eyes. But Dr. Scimonetti had a gentle vibe; he was kind and patient, and he helped me adjust.

During these visits to his office, the subject of God came up. I don't remember how, but Dr. Scimonetti sensed I was a believer.

When I said I was, he mentioned a Bible study group he had formed. Was I interested? I was.

I joined the group and soon became part of the Scimonetti family. They were among the warmest and most nourishing people I'd ever met. The Bible lessons themselves took place in Dr. Scimonetti's office every Wednesday. When I could keep up the payments on my rented Pinto, I drove over. When I relied on public transportation, I took a two-hour bus ride into the Valley. One way or another, I made it. That's how much I loved Dr. Scimonetti's teachings. I also loved how diverse the group was—from hip, young kids to older, conservative ladies. The ophthalmologist broke down the Bible with ease. And his focus was always on love.

There are preachers who preach just to hear themselves preach, preachers in love with the sound of their own voice, preachers who can't resist showing off their knowledge, preachers who like arguing down other preachers. Dr. Scimonetti was none of those. He was a preacher in the truest sense: he passionately preached the gospel, but without a hint of pretense. What's more, he never asked for anything, not a nickel. He brought Jesus to life—which, for me, is the highest form of preaching.

I'd gone to see Dr. Scimonetti out of vanity—I had to have those blue eyes I envisioned for the new character I was creating in my mind. Once I got used to the feel, I liked the look but, ironically, that look led to a renewal of my spiritual life.

Dr. Scimonetti became another father figure. I talked about him so much that out of curiosity Mom asked me to invite him to dinner at Cloverdale. He and Mom hit it off. He didn't press his spiritual beliefs on her, and she didn't press her Science of the Mind beliefs on him.

My dad, on the other hand, started challenging Dr. Scimonetti.

The Bible was filled with nonsensical stories, Dad said. Moses didn't part the Red Sea. Jesus didn't walk on water.

Dr. Scimonetti didn't protest; he never lost his composure. He simply told Dad that we were all entitled to our own interpretations. There was nothing wrong with doubt. After all, without doubt, there was no real faith.

ROMEO
AND MITZI

WHAT'S IN A NAME?

While my faith in God was reinforced, my artistic image was changing. If I was going solo, I wanted to reinvent myself, even to the point of finding a new name. Lennie Kravitz wasn't doing it for me. Lennie Kravitz sounded more like an accountant than a rock musician. *The Apprenticeship of Duddy Kravitz* had been a popular movie, with Richard Dreyfuss playing a Jewish nerd. I might have been a lot of things, but I was not a nerd. I needed something fresh.

With girls suddenly interested in me, my friends started calling me Romeo. I thought of merging "Romeo" with the name of a guitarist I admired, Adrian Belew, who'd played with Frank Zappa and Bowie. I turned "Belew" into "Blue" and came up with "Romeo Blue."

It was a name and an image that I felt fit with the glam of the early eighties. Bowie. Prince. Madonna. Romeo.

Another point: now that I had left my father's house never to return, I felt the need to change my name. It was part of my journey to figure out who I was: I had been Lennie in Manhattan; Eddie in Bed-Stuy; and Lennie in Santa Monica, Baldwin Vista, and Beverly Hills. And now, ready to forge a new path, I was Romeo Blue. And all Romeo Blue's attention was on turning out demos that would land a record deal.

I wound up at the A&M lot at La Brea and Sunset, a place heavy with Hollywood history. It had once been Charlie Chaplin's film studio. It was high energy, and its campus became my home. I crashed all night on the couches in the lounge, waking myself up just before the janitors arrived. I endeared myself to everyone, especially the secretaries and engineers. I felt that I was living in Willy Wonka's chocolate factory. It was Oz. It was where I met Quincy Jones, Bruce Swedien, and Sergio Mendes. It was where I met the Police and the Go-Go's. I met practically every artist on the A&M roster.

I worked in Studio C, just off the reception area, the smallest and cheapest space available. That little room became my laboratory. I was still experimenting with a sound that hadn't come together yet. It was just me and Dan Donnelly. He was on drums; I was on guitar, bass, and keys. Prince was still prominent in my mind, yet I was quickly coming up with original material. While it was still in a New Wave vein, it attracted at least three women at A&M who were always touting my talent: Paulette Rapp, executive assistant to Jerry Moss (the M of A&M), Iris Dillon, and Karen Clay in quality control.

When I wasn't recording my own stuff, I sat in on sessions. David Lasley, with a long, blond mane, looked like a California surfer dude but sang like a Black gospel diva. He heard me play guitar on a demo session with Siedeh Garrett, who went on to write

"Man in the Mirror" and to sing "I Just Can't Stop Loving You" with Michael Jackson. At the time, I was nineteen and David was thirty-six. He'd sung with Chic on "Good Times" and Sister Sledge on "We Are Family." He'd worked with Aretha; sung with Luther Vandross, his best friend; and toured with James Taylor for years. He'd also written "You Bring Me Joy" for Anita Baker, one of the sweetest R&B ballads.

David learned that I was living pillar to post. He didn't want me on the street and generously offered me his couch. He had written songs for everyone from Patti LaBelle to Bonnie Raitt. He had learned his craft, and he inspired me to do the same.

David thought my own songs were good enough to secure a publishing deal. He brought me over to Almo/Irving Music, the publishing arm of A&M, where I was actually signed as a writer. My first (and only) check was an advance of five thousand dollars. Five thousand!

Being my usual conservative self, I ran over to Maxfield, the store introduced to me by Lenny Steinberg, and blew all the bread on a maxi-coat by Yohji Yamamoto and a Jean-Paul Gaultier psychedelic Nehru suit. Not only was I lusting for those clothes, but I was also interested in building my Romeo Blue image. It turned out to be a timely purchase because when Herb Alpert (the A of A&M) hired me to play bass synthesizer during his *Soul Train* appearance, my look was ready.

At Almo/Irving, they gave me my own office. It was small but all mine. It had a desk with a phone, a chair, an upright piano, and a stereo system. This was it. I was being paid to write songs. I was a professional. I had twenty-four-hour access to the lot. I left my friends' names with security so they could come hang out with me at night. We'd smoke weed and listen to music until morning. It was a dream.

In the meantime, David Lasley mentored me. His songwriting tips were invaluable. So were his insights on show business. While I was living with him, he received regular late-night calls from Luther Vandross when he was back in his hotel after a show. The phone was on speaker, so I heard Luther talk about how lonely he was. It didn't matter that women all over the world were insane for him. He told David, "Child, the ladies were screaming, 'Luther! Luther!' and all I wanted to do was yell back, 'Where's your brother? Your *brother*?'" It's so sad that at that time, Luther couldn't be himself. Listening to Luther, I could hear that the magnificence of his singing voice was coming from the deepest part of his soul.

On April 1, 1984, David and I were driving down Hollywood Boulevard in his pickup truck. Michael's "Billie Jean" was blasting on the radio. Before the song was over, though, the deejay broke in to say, "Soul singer Marvin Gaye has been shot to death at his parents' home in Mid-City, Los Angeles. Reports indicate that his father, an ordained preacher, has been taken into custody as the prime suspect."

I was sure it had to be a sick April Fools' joke, but it wasn't. When I later learned that Marvin Gaye Sr. was his son's murderer, I shuddered. I knew about father-son rage. I understood how fury could turn violent. But this was an outcome beyond my imagination.

Junior high school graduation at John Adams Junior High School with my mom and Shannon Brock.

My first commercial headshot.

Graduating high school from Newbridge in L.A. with Dad.

The poster for the show my band
Wave played at Beverly Hills
High. With Kevin Conner (left)
and Tracy Oberstone.

My twenty-first birthday party at 4061
Cloverdale with Aunt Joan and Mom.

Me and Teena Marie.

Romeo Blue photo shoot, Los Angeles.

Romeo Blue photo shoot, Los Angeles.

Me, Phineas, Joey, and Tracy.

Riding the subway in New York City.

Family portrait.

Photo shoot in the backyard at home on Milwood Avenue in Venice, California.

With Jeff Ayeroff (copresident, Virgin Records), who signed me to Virgin.

Popping champagne in the shower at home in Venice with Steve Smith to celebrate the signing of my record deal with Virgin.

In the studio with my engineer Henry Hirsch.

Shooting the video for "Let Love Rule" in Central Park with my band.

My father and me at the video shoot for "Let Love Rule."

LADY T

could freeload for only so long, even off someone as gracious as David Lasley. I was always moving on. Angels appeared out of nowhere. One day, I looked up and there was Teena Marie.

As much as I liked writing songs, I was eager to get on the road and play with a real artist. That's why I auditioned to be Teena Marie's guitarist. I didn't get the gig, but Teena and I had a connection, and when her tour was over, she invited me to her home. We became friends for life.

At the time, I was nineteen, and Tina, a white singer-songwriter signed to Motown Records, was twenty-seven. When they released her debut album, *Wild and Peaceful*, the cover depicted a calm sea and a stormy sky instead of an image of the artist. Because Teena sounded so Black, Motown, aiming for a Black audience, didn't want to show her white face. Rick James, who became Teena's champion, produced the record and also sang on her hit "I'm a Sucker for Your

Love." I loved her rendition, on that same album, of "Déjà Vu, I've Been Here Before," written by Rick. When her picture appeared on her second album, *Lady T*, legions of Black fans started calling her Vanilla Child. Soon after, she appeared on Rick's *Street Songs*, singing the classic duet "Fire and Desire." She then shocked the industry by suing Motown for injuring her career by refusing to release her new material. In a landmark victory, Teena broke new ground for artists looking to leave their unsupportive labels. "Lady T," the name on the license plate of her pink '57 T-Bird convertible, was a warrior.

Teena's monster hit was "Square Biz," and her real-life manner was straight talk. She told me about being confused when, at age eight, her parents, seeing her musical talent, sent her out on the audition trail. She felt like a performing monkey. As a teen, she grew up with the gangbangers on the rough side of Venice, California. Yet Teena was all about love: she was loved by her musicians, her fans, and anyone else who came her way.

Tina would let me drive her T-Bird while, from the passenger seat, she sang and wrote songs on the spot. At the time, she was living with Rick James's sister Penny. I stayed with them for months. It was a beautiful interlude in my life. Those two women nurtured and loved me unconditionally. Teena took me to her sessions and let me sit in. She and Penny took me to Rick's house, where he'd cook his ass off for us. I also got to see Rick in the studio. Teena and Rick were self-produced visionaries. I was privileged to witness artists in command of the total studio setting. Huge lesson.

Teena also took me to my first Maze concert, at the Universal Amphitheatre, a family reunion for all Black America. When Frankie Beverly, the Maze lead singer, broke into "Happy Feelings" and "We Are One," the bond between the band and the fans became mystical. We *were* one.

Teena was my big sis, the person who kept reassuring me that though I still hadn't found my voice, I would. Because of Teena's spirit, I related to her as a Black woman. Mom loved her from the first moment they met up at Cloverdale. When we walked in, Mom was dancing by herself to Marvin Gaye's "Sexual Healing." That's all Teena needed to see. Teena knew Mom from *The Jeffersons*, and Mom knew Teena's records.

Dad was also a Teena fan. She was one of those rare people who could melt the ice between me and my father. During Cloverdale parties, Teena loved to barbecue chicken in our brick oven. She became family, ingratiating herself with Albert and Bessie, who treated her like a granddaughter.

Teena's influence helped me up my game. My demos improved. In fact, the demos I cut at A&M finally reached someone with the power to give me a deal. Miles Copeland ran I.R.S. Records. He was the brother of Police drummer Stewart Copeland and a powerful industry exec. He liked my stuff to the point that he was ready to sit down and talk business.

Whatever my problems with Dad, I knew I needed advice, so I asked him to accompany me. Sy Kravitz was hard-nosed. Nothing got by him. Miles was excited about my material. He described it as New Wave R&B. All I needed was a producer. I wasn't so sure. I wanted a deal, not a producer, but I kept quiet. Miles wanted Martin Rushent to produce me, the man who had made big hits for the Human League and the Go-Go's.

It seemed like a no-brainer, except my spirit told me it wasn't right. I can't say why. I was living in a Pinto then, and what kid living in a Pinto doesn't take a music deal? It helped that my dad had hard-core business objections to what Miles was proposing; he didn't like the terms. He was so tough, in fact, that Miles was taken aback; it was almost embarrassing. Because my album would contain all original songs, Dad insisted that I keep my publishing rights. He explained that if the record hit, publishing would be a major source of revenue. Dad's position was clear: *always hold on to your publishing.*

Copeland balked, and the deal fell apart. I wasn't all that bummed. I worried that an outside producer might mishandle my music. I also realized that Dad was right. When you write a song, the publishing rights inherently belong to you. Why give them away? Yet scores of artists, thrilled by the idea of being signed, do just that. That's the moment when record labels feed off artists' vulnerability. Fortunately, in that moment of vulnerability, Dad protected me.

All this meant that I was still on the loose, still looking for a sound, a voice, a deal.

Mom supported my search. But I didn't make it easy for her. She had her heart set on my going to Howard, her alma mater. She was the first in her family to graduate college. Grandpa Albert made the same point: look at what Black people had sacrificed so that a kid like me could get ahead. These ideas were coming from the two people who had shaped my character and molded my morals. For them, education was everything. Mom had done graduate work abroad. Grandpa had devoted his life to learning. The fact that I wasn't about to continue my formal education hurt them. I wish I could have prevented that hurt, but my focus never changed—it was music or nothing.

The collapse of the I.R.S. deal didn't hurt my hustle. I was still on the grind, still convinced it was only a matter of time. Besides, others believed in me. One big believer was Kennedy Gordy, who called to say he'd written a surefire hit that was perfect for my style. I had to hear it right away.

I was up at Cloverdale visiting Mom when Kennedy came over carrying a LinnDrum machine, a keyboard, and an amp. He played and sang "Somebody's Watching Me." I liked it, it was really good, but I didn't feel it was right for me. He asked me to think it over. Kennedy was Berry Gordy's son. Berry was a star-maker. Berry could sign anyone he wanted. Motown was the big leagues. Was I stupid to turn this down?

A few weeks later, Kennedy recorded the song himself, using the name Rockwell. Berry Gordy, the man who signed, produced, and broke the Jackson 5, got Michael Jackson to sing on the chorus, and "Somebody's Watching Me" became an international smash.

I'm a little amazed how much stuff I turned down at a time when I was so determined to make it. What do I attribute that to? What was I thinking? I wasn't thinking. I was reacting. My gut simply said no.

As time went on, more opportunities would come my way, and I'd continue to turn down songs that had success written all over them. It wasn't arrogance that made me pass over those opportunities. I wasn't ego-tripping. If anything, it was the opposite. I never forgot one of my mother's favorite admonitions: self-praise is no recommendation.

No, it was simply that the opportunities presented to me up until that point hadn't allowed me to be my true self. I always knew that if I couldn't express my musical soul, I wouldn't be worth a damn.

LIPTON AND LOVE

After moving to California nine years earlier, my family continued flying back to New York for regular visits. Now I started going back on my own. Practically every month, I ran over to LAX and bought a ninety-nine-dollar ticket to JFK on a budget airline called People Express. With money saved from odd jobs and studio gigs, I zipped back and forth like it was a bus ride.

In New York, I returned to Brooklyn, where Grandma and Grandpa had kept their house at the corner of Throop Avenue and Kosciuszko Street. There was always a room there for me. Over in Manhattan, I stayed with the Bernsteins (my pal Adam and his dad, promoter Sid Bernstein) at their palatial pad at 1000 Park Avenue. Never wanting to overstay my welcome, though, I kept moving on. When none of my old Upper East Side pals was around to let me crash in their parents' apartment, I slept on the floor of friends' East Village lofts. I was all over the place.

I wound up in New Jersey because of Tisha Campbell. We had kept in touch since *The Me Nobody Knows*, and I couldn't wait to see her again. She was a couple of years younger than me but already a pro, a gorgeous young woman who could act, sing, and dance with the confidence of someone twice her age. I was in love with her voice. I saw Tisha as a songstress, and I wanted to write and produce for her.

The attraction between us was so strong that, within weeks, I wound up living in her family home in East Orange, just outside Newark, the city where she'd been raised. It was cramped quarters. The household included Tisha's mom, singer Mona Raye; her aunt Sharon; Sharon's son, Eddie; and Tisha's three brothers, Taye, Jermaine, and Stanley. The whole family accepted me, although her mother didn't want me sleeping in the room with her daughter. But because Mona Raye had gigs, she was gone evenings, giving us time to slip into the bedroom to hang out. When it was time to turn in, instead of saying, "Go to bed, Lenny," Tisha's aunt Sharon would quip, "Go to floor." The cold-ass wooden floor was my bed.

A few times, Tisha and I went to Mr. G's, the nightclub where Mona Raye held court. The woman could sing. When she did Billie Holiday's "God Bless the Child," I thought of my own mother. It was Mom's favorite song and one of her mantras: *God bless the child that's got his own*. The soul got even deeper when Mona Raye called Tisha up to a sing a duet.

Mona had put Tisha together with Reggie Lucas, a Jersey-based producer who had worked with Madonna. I had different ideas about the direction I thought she should take. I saw her more as Whitney than Madonna. But Mona was happy with the way things were. Why should Tisha listen to me when she had a professional producer with hits under his belt? I didn't even have a belt.

Despite our differences of opinion, I loved living in East Orange. Tisha's household was wild. People coming and going night and day. It was fun. At times, there wasn't much food in the house. Tisha's brothers would battle over the last couple of slices of bologna. We had to improvise. We'd open a cabinet, grab a box of Kraft Macaroni and Cheese, and drop in the seasoning packets from a box of Lipton Onion Soup. It filled our stomachs, and it actually tasted good. Tisha and I lived on Lipton and love.

Like me, Tisha was looking to live a creative life. She was a free spirit with a beautiful heart. Just to be with her and her family, I braved the long haul from New York, taking subways, the PATH train to Jersey, and the trolley to East Orange.

One haul threw me for a loop. On my way home from the city, I was about to put in a token to catch the PATH train when I realized I was broke. No big deal. Just jump the turnstile. It was an easy leap, and I landed on both feet. That's when someone grabbed me by the neck. I turned around. It was a cop, and he had only one word for me: "Busted." He'd caught me red-handed the very week the local mayor was making an example of fare dodgers.

The next thing I knew I was inside a paddy wagon and handcuffed to a drug addict who had just shit his pants. I nearly choked on the stink. The traffic was slow. The stink got worse. The ride to headquarters took forever. Booking took another two hours. I asked to make a call. The person I knew to call was the same person I didn't want to call: my father. I knew he had the connections I needed, but I also knew I'd have to eat crow. Not only would I have to say that I was in jail, but I'd have to explain why.

Nonetheless, I did what I had to do. I called Dad and, much to my shock, he was cool. No lectures, no rebukes, no yelling. He called his friend Barry Slotnick, a well-respected criminal lawyer famous for successfully defending Mafia bosses. I wondered if he'd met Slotnick through Uncle Vinnie.

However he'd met Slotnick, Slotnick pulled it off. Within an hour, the attorney got me out with a small fine.

Thank you, Mr. Slotnick.

Thank you, Dad.

There was just one hiccup: while I was in custody, the jail's computer system went down. That meant that no matter what, they couldn't release me. I had to spend the night in the can.

I have a feeling my father's willingness to help actually made him feel good. He got to show me, his rebellious son, that he had power. He could pull strings and get me out of scrapes. No matter how much I might resent him, I still needed him. I had needed him to encourage me to become a solo artist, and I had needed him to keep me from selling away my publishing. I didn't like admitting it, but I needed him in many ways.

Back on the streets, I borrowed some money, paid the train fare, and finally got to East Orange. Tisha and I carried on for months. Then she landed a gig in England as one of the three Supreme-like singers in the film version of *Little Shop of Horrors*. Later, she was also cast as a lead in Spike Lee's *School Daze*. Her career was off and running, but in a direction that led her away from me. We remained close, but the love light faded, and soon we broke up.

Back in the city, things were grim. Despite my web of friends, my couch-surfing luck had run out. I'd spend days and nights riding the subway from the Bronx to Lower Manhattan. With money low and winter coming on strong, I had to think fast.

One slate-gray winter day in 1983, I wasn't loving the city. I was in between crash pads. The air was frigid, the wind blowing hard off the Hudson. I was in my usual outfit of jeans, a denim jacket, and a raggedy scarf, and even in the January snow, I was still wearing sandals with white tube socks. I hadn't shaved in weeks—I've never been big on shaving—and my nappy hair was contained by an oversize woolen cap. As the snow started falling, I dreamed of the Bahamian sun. I'd used up my friends' favors and needed to figure out my next move. I was essentially homeless. But this was nothing new—being nomadic was my way of life—and I wasn't worried. Maybe that's because I knew my folks would never let me starve. I had nothing, but I lived in an abundant world. My job was to follow the music.

That's why I was walking down Forty-Eighth Street toward the music stores. It didn't matter that the snowfall was getting heavier. It didn't matter that my feet were getting soaked or that the bitterly cold wind was freezing my face. Once inside Manny's, where Dad bought me my first guitar, I'd be home. Many of the old clerks at Manny's had known me since I was a seven-year-old begging them to let me stroke every guitar and beat every drum. Now I worked my way down the street, stopping at all the shops, first Manny's and then Sam Ash.

I was checking out a Voyetra-8, a complex synthesizer, when this dude came over and said, "Don't buy it." He explained that it didn't have MIDI. He further explained that MIDI stood for Musical Instrument Digital Interface. MIDI was the future, he said. With lightning speed, it could transfer digital signals to layer or separate sounds through multiple channels and ports. Basically, MIDI allowed different systems to talk to one another.

I asked if he was in a band. He said yes, the Michael Zager Band. I knew their disco hit "Let's All Chant." It turned out he'd written the song and sung lead vocals on the record. He introduced himself as Alvin Fields. I introduced myself as Romeo Blue. He looked at my soaking wet sandals, thought for a minute, and asked if I happened to be the same cat in the long coat who'd played bass synth with Herb Albert on *Soul Train*. I beamed. Yes, that was me!

Sensing that I might be homeless, Alvin asked if I had a place to stay. I didn't. So, he invited me to crash at his place, at 111 West Ninety-Fourth Street. It was a tiny studio apartment dominated by an enormous widescreen television and a battery of keyboards, drum machines, and sequencers. Of course, he had a full-on MIDI system.

Within minutes, we went to work. We played for hours. At some point, after Alvin showed me the intricacies of his system, he told me about how he had produced Cissy Houston while her daughter Whitney stood on a milk crate singing background. On Alvin's bookshelf, I noticed a *Playbill* from the early 1970s of the original Broadway production of *The Me Nobody Knows*. I told him I had been in the revival. He asked me if I knew Tisha Campbell. Are you kidding me?

Crazy small world.

I asked Alvin if I could use his phone. I called Tisha and said, "There's someone here who'd like to talk to you." I put Alvin on and heard Tisha scream, "Alvin!" It was fun to listen to them catch up after so long. After Alvin hung up, I said, "Why don't we write a song for her? I really believe in her voice. Maybe we can put some tunes together that would help her get a deal." The Reggie Lucas thing had never come to fruition, but I knew Tisha had "it."

A few days later, in the middle of working with Alvin on Tisha's song, I said, "Yo, can we take a break to watch *The Jeffersons*?" He said, "Sure, why?" When I told him why, he was amazed I hadn't mentioned who my mother was earlier. There was no reason to, I said; now there was. The next day, I called Mom to say I'd finally found a place to stay. She wanted to know where and with whom, and immediately asked to speak with Alvin.

We were watching *The Miss America Pageant*. "Alvin, my mom wants to speak with you." He got on the phone, introduced himself, and respectfully answered all Mom's questions. He gave her his phone number and address and assured her that he didn't do drugs and that he would look out for me. When he convinced Mom that I was staying in a sane and safe place, she sounded relieved. Alvin handed me the phone, and I told her I'd be in touch. As we hung up, the winner was crowned. It was Vanessa Williams.

I learned that before I came to live with Alvin, his roommate had been Jean-Michel Basquiat. Alvin said that Jean-Michel and I had similar energy. I hadn't met the painter, but I knew his work well enough to understand that Alvin was giving me major props.

Alvin and I completed our song for Tisha. It was called "Love Is the Only Key." Tisha came by to cut a demo right there in his tiny apartment. There was barely room for the three of us to move. Alvin and I played all the instruments and sang background. Tisha brought it home with a brilliant lead vocal.

So, I got my wish of making music for Tisha. Unfortunately, nothing happened with the tune. As far as I'm concerned, it was a hit in an alternate universe. Tisha leaned more into acting instead and ultimately landed a huge role costarring with Martin Lawrence on *Martin*.

While still living at Alvin's, I happened to glance at a cover of *TV Guide* featuring the cast of *The Cosby Show*. I pointed to Lisa Bonet and calmly said, "I'm gonna marry that girl." Alvin laughed. *The Cosby Show* was at its height of popularity, presenting a vision of upper-class Black life that Reagan's America was willing to embrace. Father Cliff Huxtable was an obstetrician; mother Clair was a lawyer; and the kids, except for one, were straight arrows. That "one" was Denise, played by Lisa. Denise was different, and I knew, just by watching the show, that Lisa was different as well.

I'd spent a lot of my life hanging around sitcoms. I knew the genre demanded broad comedic skills. Its masters—Lucille Ball, Jackie Gleason, Red Foxx—found ways to humanize stereotypes: a whacky housewife, a frustrated bus driver, a junkyard owner. Supporting cast members usually didn't demonstrate the complexities of the central characters. But on *The Cosby Show*, the reverse was true. Denise/Lisa was the most fascinating family member. She stood apart and seemed to be living some secret inner life. She had a come-hither magnetism that drove boys and men mad. She was a bohemian dreamer wrapped in mysterious allure. I wanted to solve that mystery—or at least get close to it.

But how in the world could that ever happen?

SHOCK

The ninety-nine-dollar People Express had dropped me back in L.A. I got off the plane and drove over to Cloverdale to grab some things. Dad didn't hear me come in. Mom was in Nassau visiting Esau. Walking down the hall, I could hear Dad talking on the phone in his bedroom. I can't tell you why, but something about the tone of his voice made me walk toward his door to listen in.

I started to make out what he was saying:

"Baby, baby . . ."

I inched closer and closer. I knew he wasn't talking to my mother. I had never heard him call her "baby," and if he had, it sure as hell wouldn't have been in that tone of voice.

I continued eavesdropping and heard him say, "I can't hide the last fifty thousand."

I stopped breathing. My throat went dry. My heart started racing. I stayed frozen in place, listening to every word of his conversation. My ears caught fire. The more he talked, the more I realized he was talking to a *girlfriend*. I couldn't make out every word, but I definitely got the gist: he was cheating on Mom and supporting his mistress with Mom's money.

I went beyond anger. I was on the verge of exploding. The first thing that came to my mind was the gun Dad kept hidden in his closet. I know that's crazy, but that's how I was thinking. He was betraying my mother, the woman who honored and loved him with all her heart, the woman who'd stood by him through thick and thin. All the fury I'd been feeling for my father since I was a little boy, two decades of pent-up rage, erupted inside my head. I wanted to kill him. Right then and there, I wanted him dead.

It was only the grace of God that checked that instinct. Every second of every minute of every hour of every day that I had spent praying to the Lord of love came to fruition in that very moment. I couldn't ignore the words that God spoke to me then. They couldn't have been clearer.

Don't do it.

"Thank you, God," I said silently. I went back to my room, picked up the phone, and made a call.

My cousin Esau answered.

"Esau," I said, "please put Mom on the phone."

Mom heard that I was alarmed, but I couldn't tell her why— not now. I had to do it in person. I asked her to buy me a ticket so I could fly to Nassau that very night. She kept asking why. I said, "You're gonna have to trust me. It's an emergency. And if you don't send me down there, somebody might die."

I could hear Mom's voice trembling with fright as she said, "I'll call you right back with the details."

A few hours later, I was on the red-eye from LAX to Miami. Flying across the country, I found thoughts flying across my mind: *Why would he? How could he? How dare he! Who is she? What does she look like? How old is she? How long has it been going on? What makes him think he can get away with it? That son of a bitch. That asshole. That cheater. All this time, trying to be a Hollywood big shot, only to live off his wife's success, only to end up double-crossing the woman who means more to me than anyone.*

I landed in Miami. A sudden storm meant the prop plane to Nassau was delayed. I tried to sleep in the airport waiting area. But sleep wouldn't come. The thoughts wouldn't stop. I stared out at the pouring rain. Lightning streaked the sky. Then the sky gave way to golden sun as the rain turned to a gentle shower. I thought of Grandma Bessie. When it was sunny and raining at the same time, she always used to say, "The devil is beating his wife."

Angry thoughts returned. Two cups of coffee. Then I jumped on the little prop plane and flew over a strangely calm sea—still feeling unsettled, still feeling crazy.

Mom met me at the airport. We drove to the Britannia Beach Hotel on Paradise Island, where, in a little courtyard, we sat down. She looked at me. I looked at her. I was an emotional mess. With no sleep and after traveling across the country, I had to drop a bomb that would destroy my mother's world.

The silence was deafening.

I laid out the story.

I said, "Dad is having an affair with a woman, and I believe he's stealing your money and giving it to her."

At that moment, I saw something I'd never seen before. I saw my mother's face crack and her soul fall to the floor. I watched the life drain from her body. She became an empty shell. She didn't move, didn't cry, didn't even respond. Her eyes were vacant. After a few minutes, she found her composure and began speaking.

She told me that my father had been cheating throughout their marriage. She told me how she'd have to go to his mistresses' apartments when I was an infant and, with me in her arms, buzz the intercom to tell the woman, "Tell Sy that playtime's over. Time to come home."

She also told me how Grandpa Joe Kravitz had repeatedly cheated on Grandma Jean, and how Sy had hated his father for it. It was history repeating itself.

I asked Mom why she hadn't left Dad. She shared that she was a committed wife. Her Bahamian upbringing was ironclad: divorce was not an option. She was determined, largely because of me, to keep this marriage together. Besides, Dad had promised to change. The promise wasn't kept. There were a few more indiscretions, but they were short-lived. She had thought he'd finally mended his ways. This was the first time she'd shared this intimate information with me.

I asked her what she was going to do. She explained that, for now, it was best to do nothing—not say a word, not let Dad know that she knew. She'd return to L.A. and act like everything was normal. Meanwhile, she'd hire professionals to document his affair. When she confronted him, she would be armed with incontrovertible proof. And the only way to obtain that proof was to make sure he remained in the dark.

In a remarkably short period of time, Mom's mood had changed. Ten minutes before, she had been crushed. Now she had a plan.

A few days later, Mom and I returned home. She went back to Cloverdale. To feel safe, she suggested that I stay in the house for another week. That's how I got to see what I consider the greatest dramatic performance of her life.

She greeted Dad warmly. She acted as though nothing were wrong. She laughed at his jokes. She slept in their bed. She fixed his breakfast. And all the while, she showed no anger, resentment, or suspicion.

Meanwhile, she had hired a private detective. It didn't take long. Three weeks later, she received a folder with incriminating pictures, bank statements, and receipts that included two round-trip tickets to Paris on the Concorde.

When it was time for the big confrontation, I listened from the living room, adjacent to the master bedroom wall. I heard screaming, hysteria. I heard Mom saying, "How could you go into our finances to keep a mistress?" She shoved a folder of photographs and papers in his face, proof that he had paid for the girl's college tuition, her rent on a Westwood apartment, and the monthly note on her Mercedes. The "girl" was a young Black woman in her early twenties who, ironically, worked at their bank.

When Mom mentioned the Concorde tickets to Paris, she completely lost it. She screamed that he'd been promising to take *her* to Paris for years, only to learn he had taken a secret trip there with his girlfriend. She was beyond furious.

Instead of begging forgiveness, Dad, in shock, was stone-cold silent. No explanation, no apology, no remorse, no nothing. He was paralyzed.

Mom stayed strong throughout the ordeal.

Being as private as she was, she told only a couple of friends, who gave her some comfort and support. Regardless of how hurt and mortified she was, her intention had been to somehow still make the marriage work. For Roxie Roker, through love, there was always a solution.

Then she learned something that took that possibility away.

She received an ominous phone call from someone in Las Vegas concerning a large sum of money owed by Dad. Knowing that Dad liked hanging around wiseguys, she reasoned that it was time to cut all ties with him. She was frightened that Dad had possibly put the family in danger. She wanted nothing to do with his gambling debts or anyone looking to collect. She filed for divorce. She wanted distance between him and us. She wanted him out.

She wanted him out so badly, in fact, that as she was saying all this to me, he was in the bedroom packing. When he came into the living room, suitcases in hand, she asked if he had anything to tell his son. Meanwhile, this man still didn't know that I was the one who'd given Mom the information that had led us to this moment. It was her final hope that he might say something redeeming, an apology. That he would let me know how wrong he had been, so that I, in turn, might learn from his tragic mistakes.

Silence.

At least thirty seconds ticked by. Dad looked away from me. I had no idea what he would say. What *could* he say? My heart was beating. My throat was dry. Finally, after what seemed an eternity, he raised his head and looked me dead in the eyes before saying the words that would haunt me for the rest of my life:

"You'll do it, too."

"WHO THE FUCK DO YOU THINK YOU ARE TO TURN DOWN A DEAL LIKE THIS?"

Before discovering that Dad was cheating, I had viewed his relationship with Mom as good. I was naïve. For all my problems with my father, I never saw him as deceitful. Just as Mom had been undyingly loyal to him, I had presumed he was loyal to her. Their bond seemed indestructible. I never saw the cracks in the façade. So, when the façade crumbled, I realized I had been ignoring the warning signs.

I should have put two and two together when Jewel told me her pimp thought she could use me to meet Dad. Obviously, Dad had a reputation. But I wasn't thinking about Dad back then. I was thinking about helping Jewel. Proof of that reputation came when Phineas Newborn and Joey Collins learned that my parents had split up. They weren't surprised. They had once seen Dad out with another woman.

Why hadn't they told me?

Because they didn't want to hurt me. Or hurt Mom.

In the aftermath of the divorce, I was willing to stay at Cloverdale, but Mom knew there was no turning back the clock. I had to move on with my life. She helped by paying the security deposit on a small place in the Hollywood Hills. My roommate was Christopher Enuke, a Nigerian educated in England whom I had met through Eliza Steinberg's mom, Lenny. Christopher had flair. Four years older than me, he was a star student at Otis Art Institute of Parsons School of Design.

We rented an old Hollywood Hills two-bedroom house. The thing stood on stilts and offered a gorgeous view of the city. Because the rent sapped all our money, we had no furniture other than mattresses. We didn't even have a car, and we had to trek down the hill for thirty minutes just to get to the grocery store. Our meals were sparse: roasted potatoes glazed with honey, white Japanese rice with seaweed.

I had my instruments; Christopher had his drafting table—and for a while, that was enough. We spent our days and nights honing our crafts. Our landlady, Marty Costanza, an attractive older woman, put up with our rent being constantly late every month in exchange for our shameless flirtations. Christopher and I would argue over whose turn it was to go over to her place to charm her into giving us more time.

Christopher made his own clothes and let me wear them: leather pants and jackets, kilts, and jewelry made from the scraps. He had great taste and was also a ladies' man with the charming arrogance of an African prince.

One evening, Christopher wanted to give me a present. He

knew a beautiful woman willing to love me for a night. When she came over, I didn't know the arrangement. I said hello and went upstairs to listen to music. The next thing I knew, she'd come into my room and was taking off all her clothes. She said, "I'm a gift from Christopher." As fine as she was, I just couldn't do it.

When Christopher graduated Otis Parsons in 1984, I threw him a big party. With whatever little money I had, I got this soul food catering company to come up to the house with a feast: fried chicken, cornbread, collard greens, macaroni and cheese—the whole lot. And, yes, watermelon. All his friends and classmates showed up. When Christopher walked in, I was so excited to see his reaction.

Being a Nigerian with an English boarding school upringing, he didn't get it. Here was the school's star student at his big, fancy graduation celebration, and there I was embarrassing him with this pickaninny nigger food. By evening's end, though, he was over it, dancing with his friends and eating the damn chicken.

Christopher's future in fashion was a sure thing, but our life as roommates in the Hollywood Hills didn't last long. We ran out of money and started spinning in different directions.

Meanwhile, I kept pushing my music. I'd ask myself, *Who am I and what do I want to say?* I still didn't have any answers.

I was still Romeo Blue.

I was still without a sound I could live with.

I was still without a group I could call my own.

I was still searching.

Searching meant jamming. When in doubt, I found that my default position was always to jam. Jamming is its own reward. So, I kept jamming with the best musicians from Beverly, like guitarist

Vadim Zilberstein, bassist Osama Afifi, keyboardist Don Wyatt, and bassist Kevin Wyatt.

On the streets, at backyard parties, and at all-night sessions in the studio, I kept at it. I sought out the wisdom of my godmothers and other elders like Linda Hopkins, the epic soul singer. I had seen Linda in *Me and Bessie* on Broadway when I was a kid. She was Mom's friend and then became my friend as well. Linda was the real deal: a raw, romping blues singer and a direct link to the ancient heritage of Black music. I loved the times I spent in her vibey little apartment, where she'd cook for me amid her coterie of adoring gay boyfriends.

I also sought out producers like John Barnes, an eloquent brother with sleepy red eyes, a thick mustache, and a bass-bottom voice. He was the young wiz who'd played on "We Are the World" for Lionel Richie and Michael Jackson, who'd helped put together "Liberian Girl" on Michael's *Bad* album, and who'd worked with Diana Ross and Julio Iglesias. Among the first to master the Synclavier, John designed complex musical constructions like an architect.

John gave Romeo Blue a big break when I co-produced disco diva Thelma Houston singing "What a Woman Feels Inside." I also played guitar on the track. I arranged it as a straight-up R&B ballad, but John modernized it with a heavy dose of Synclavier that, to my ears, undercut the feel. Nevertheless, MCA dug it and placed it on Thelma's album, *Qualifying Heat.*

John and I kept at it. I studied his techniques at the board. I was in awe of his talent. His work ethic more than matched mine, but it was fueled by cocaine. He was hardly alone. The snow blizzard of the eighties blanketed the music industry. Pot was a mellow high. Coke was anything but mellow. The drug triggered a frenetic energy that separated me from my soul. I didn't judge snorters. I just didn't like the shit they were snorting.

After one all-night session when John was wired, we went out for breakfast. We were driving through Hollywood when a cop pulled us over. We weren't speeding, we hadn't been drinking, and, for once, I wasn't holding any weed. I wasn't worried, but John was. I understood why when the cops found a huge bag of coke in the backseat. They said they were taking us both in. John was a stand-up guy, though: he insisted the coke was his, not mine, and just like that I was set free. John was hauled off to the station while I drove around in his car and arranged his bail.

I could picture my parents' reaction if I'd been arrested for drugs. It was only John Barnes's integrity that kept my young ass out of jail.

More searching, more jamming, more musicians.

Tony LeMans was crazy talented. I met him back in junior high, when his name was Tony Fortier. Like me, he had reinvented himself in an attempt to break into the business. In terms of looks, we could have been brothers. Tony had played French horn in Miss Beasley's orchestra. We'd lost track of each other until he showed up at the Wave concert at Beverly Hills High. He, too, was searching for the right sound. Since I'd seen him last, he'd made big strides as a writer and singer. He'd grown his hair out and looked like a rock star. Tony modeled himself after Sly Stone. We shared a passion for old-school funk.

Tony was the partner I'd been looking for. He had style and swag. On a personal level, there was always an undercurrent of competition coming from Tony, but I avoided side-by-side comparisons by lavishly praising him. The praise was genuine. He had laser-like focus.

At first, I was Tony's wingman. We were working on material that featured him. It was basically funk with intricate background harmonies. Although digital synthesizers, drum machines, and sequencers were what was happening, Tony and I were cultivating a sound that harkened back to the old school—kind of Sly meets the Beatles.

Because I was still hanging out at A&M, I knew John McClain, the record man who'd launched Janet Jackson's career with a genius move: putting her with producer-songwriters Jimmy Jam and Terry Lewis. An industry powerhouse, John had grown up with the Jacksons and eventually became coexecutor of Michael's estate.

When John heard our demos, he loved our vibe. He wanted to take it even further. His idea was to group me and Tony with three other musicians and form a Black Duran Duran. He'd break us out in Europe and then bring us home, where we'd be greeted as superstars. We couldn't miss. A boy band chased down by hordes of screaming fans.

My bandmates were wild for the idea. I wasn't. I wasn't sure I wanted to go that route. McClain came on strong. He called us into his lavish office, which looked like an apartment, the walls lined with gold and platinum records. Right there on the spot, he offered us a deal. My bandmates were salivating and ready to sign. I wasn't. They got furious with me. McClain got even more furious.

"Who the fuck do you think you are to turn down a deal like this?" he yelled.

I didn't have an answer. My refusal made no sense to him. Struggling musicians don't turn down deals with major labels, especially with someone as powerful as John. But deep down, I knew it just wasn't what I wanted to do.

Except for Tony, my bandmates went their own way. Tony and I stuck together. If a Black Duran Duran didn't fit our style, we'd find something that would.

Up stepped Benny Medina, a music exec I'd met years earlier at the Gordy mansion, where as a teenager he ran errands for Berry. A sharp guy, Benny had worked his way up to become A&R head at Motown before switching to Warner Bros. Records. In fact, Will Smith's character in *The Prince of Bel-Air* was based on Benny and his early life.

When Tony and I played the demos we'd made, Benny thought we had serious potential. He saw us as a funkier version of Hall and Oates. We took that as a compliment. Benny gave us a development deal that allowed us to go back into the studio and cut more tunes. Warner Bros. also put us up at the Oakwood apartments, where out-of-town musicians and actors stayed while working in L.A. We each bought a motorcycle—Honda Rebels, poor man's Harleys—and we were off and running! The songwriting went well. We were cranking out demos on a regular basis. We switched off on vocals, switched off on instruments, and generated some material. So far, so good. Then Sly Stone came to town.

Sly actually moved into the Oakwood. I was thrilled to meet him. He was one of the titans. I'd watch him coming out of his apartment dressed to the nines, with a woman on each arm. Both Tony and I idolized Sly. But Tony took it even further. He wanted to *embody* Sly; he wanted to *be* him. I was cool just seeing Sly around the complex, but Tony started seeking him out, and then hanging regularly in his apartment. Then Tony disappeared for days, which turned into weeks. Come to find out, they were bingeing on crack together. Our production came to a screeching halt. Eventually, though, Tony showed up to do some work.

Then came another problem: a beautiful girl named Sonia. I'd met her in Nassau when my cousin Jennifer got married. Sonia was smart, gorgeous, irresistible. I fell hard, really hard. I ran up a huge phone bill keeping in touch with her, until I finally convinced her to come to L.A. to stay with me at the Oakwood. She met Tony and, for a few days, everything was cool. Then came the afternoon when Tony and Sonia hopped on his bike to grab food. I was fine with that—until they didn't return that night. Or the next night. Or the night after.

I was really scared that something had happened. Did they get in an accident? Were they alive? I didn't think in a million years that Tony would steal my girl. But that's exactly what he did. When they finally showed up three days later, their lame explanation was that they'd been exploring Malibu. I was heartbroken. I really loved this girl. But to Tony, she was just a plaything. I told Sonia I couldn't do this. She had to leave. I booked her a flight back to Nassau and rode her to LAX on my bike. Saying good-bye hurt.

But music is a powerful force—so powerful that, in spite of his stealing my girl, Tony and I stuck together. I hung in with him. We went back to making demos. We put together a live showcase that I co-produced. I played bass and backed Tony while he sang lead. Sheila E., who had hit it big with "The Glamorous Life" and was the opening act for the *Purple Rain* tour, told Prince about us. Prince signed Tony, who wanted me as part of the deal. Prince told Tony that although his shit was funky, the recordings didn't sound like professional records, and that he'd need a producer. I completely disagreed. The rawness was one of the chief elements that defined Tony.

Prince had a vision of Tony that was smoother and more synthetic. Thus, he hired producer David Gamson. A multi-instrumentalist, Gamson was one half of British duo Scritti Politti and composer of most of their massive hits. He was king of the synths. Look, I loved Scritti, I had their CD, but to me that sound had nothing to do with Tony.

Still, Tony drank the Kool-Aid. His funk got diluted. He was convinced cleaning up his sound would mean commercial success. Desperately searching for a smash, he rushed into the synth pop era directed by a man who helped define that era. When Tony's Gamson-produced album on Prince's Paisley Park Records was released, I was still rooting for him. I genuinely wanted him to succeed. The album was clean and professional and Tony sang his ass off. But when the record didn't sell, and the songs, caught in that techno bubble, already sounded dated, I realized one thing for sure: you can't fuck with your musical DNA without losing something sacred. I was still looking for the sacred. And not even a figure as imposing as Prince could convince me it was there when my heart said it wasn't.

A few years later, while working on a second album, Tony died in a tragic accident on the Pacific Coast Highway in Malibu. That broke my heart. For all that had gone down between us, I still thought of Tony as my brother and a man of enormous talent. I only wish the world had the opportunity to hear the pure musical spirit that I knew lived deep within his soul.

COLLEGE

I didn't go to college, but I did. That is, on a regular basis, I'd go visit my friends at college. Eliza Steinberg and Jane Greenberg were back east, calling and writing about how they loved their schools. I had to see for myself.

It was the mid-eighties. Jane was at Bennington, in Vermont. The whole setting appealed to me: the kicked-back campus, the leafy trees, the coeds in tie-dyed skirts, the professors in tweedy sport coats. It was great being back with Jane. It was also great jamming with the local musicians. It was at Bennington where I met Bret Easton Ellis, whose novel *Less Than Zero* was all about the drug-crazed children of the idle rich. A few months later, I was at Bret's publication party in Manhattan, where I met, for the one and only time, Andy Warhol. The pop art painter made a grand appearance with two statuesque African models. Blond-wigged Andy was the king, and they were his queens. I secretly wished that one day I'd be featured in Andy's *Interview* magazine, but it never happened. I saw Andy as a rebel who'd defied tradition. Jane said that he actually had a degree in fine arts from Carnegie Tech. Andy Warhol had gone to college.

Deep down, I had some feelings about *not* having gone to college. After all, my folks were college graduates. Walking around Bennington, seeing the kids with their backpacks stuffed with books, I knew I was missing something. I knew there was something invaluable about a formal education. By skipping college, I wondered if I was shortchanging myself. At the same time, I knew I could never focus on academics. I couldn't sit still long enough to get even a semester under my belt. I was too restless, too eager to make it as a musician.

I loved Bard as much as Bennington. Bard was where Eliza was studying—and also where Donald Fagen had met Walter Becker and eventually formed Steely Dan. Eliza let me sit in on her classes, took me to parties, and introduced me to her beautiful friend Ming See Lau, nicknamed Mitzi.

Mitzi spoke with a soft, enchanting Chinese British accent. She was worldly, sensuous, smart, and deep into music and fashion. Though she was the daughter of a wealthy businessman, she wasn't spoiled or pretentious. Her charm was as natural as her love for the arts. From that first night we met at Bard, we couldn't see enough of each other. We fell into a whirlwind romance. And it all started at college.

Soon, our lives became intertwined. When she wasn't at school, she stayed at her apartment, in a doorman building at 200 East Fifty-Seventh Street, off Third Avenue. She invited me to move in, and suddenly I was back in the vicinity of my early childhood, affluent Manhattan.

Mitzi took me to a boutique that carried clothes by cutting-edge designers: Charivari, on West Fifty-Seventh. Given that I didn't have much of a wardrobe, she sweetly clothed me in the latest fashions. We were young and genuinely in love, but Mitzi became somewhat of a benefactor. I had mixed feelings about that. Part of me would rather have paid my own bills, but another part liked having a girl-friend who was happy making me happy. Mitzi had no qualms about helping me pursue my musical dreams.

Mitzi and I flew to L.A., where she leased us a loft downtown that appealed to the New Yorker in me. This was way before the area got hip. In a refurbished warehouse on the corner of Seventh and Alameda, the loft looked down on the Greyhound bus station where the homeless camped out in a dingy waiting room.

A young architect and graphic designer, Michael Czysz, lived in the same building, in a loft with concrete floors. Those floors inspired me to do the same. In one of my first design projects, I laid chicken wire over my wooden floors and poured the concrete myself. The result was unsafe, rough but right.

Our loft was big enough to house a small studio I'd built with the brand-new Akai 12-track board. It was all open space: kitchen, bedroom, and living room. I was constantly in the studio, still looking for the sound that kept eluding me. After hours of making music or late nights with Mitzi, we'd go to Gorky's, a cafeteria spe-cializing in Russian omelets.

The life of the Gemini went on: a week in seedy downtown L.A. buying fifty-cent burritos from a food truck, followed by a week in Manhattan dining at Le Cirque on the Upper East Side.

My essential nature, living high while living low, hadn't changed. What had changed was that I'd come of age.

TWENTY-ONE

M om had been throwing me birthday parties since I was one. No matter what else was happening in my life, it was a ritual I looked forward to.

Twenty-one is a milestone, and Mom wanted to mark it with fanfare. She was living in Cloverdale—without Dad, of course—and saw no reason that Cloverdale shouldn't be the place. It was, and will always be, where the family came together to celebrate.

For all the love surrounding me, the night turned out strange and a little strained. Naturally, I dressed for the occasion: a suit by Yohji with a print that looked like splattered paint. The guests included friends of my folks, plus Grandpa Albert and Grandma Bessie; choir buddies Phineas and Joey; Tony LeMans; Dan Donnelly; Kennedy Gordy; David Lasley and Teena Marie; my godmothers Joan Hamilton Brooks, Diahann Carroll, and Joy Homer. And then there was Jewel, looking healthy and strong. Being compassionate, Mom had reached out and invited her.

I wondered if Dad would show up. When he did, I had mixed emotions. He walked around and chatted with everyone as though he still lived there. And he talked and laughed with Mom as if nothing had happened. They both looked beautiful, and for a moment I wished that things could go back to the way they were. I'm sure he wished that, too.

After I blew out the twenty-one candles, it was time for my big announcement:

Mitzi and I were engaged!

I'd bought her an antique ring. I hoped Mom would be pleased, but I saw that she was taken by surprise. I hadn't discussed it with her. Mitzi was sweet, educated, and responsible, but I'm sure that in Mom's eyes we were too young. Dad remained stone silent.

Over the coming months, Mitzi and my mother grew close. Meanwhile, in Hong Kong, the Laus were not happy. I don't think they were into having an unemployed Black musician as a son-in-law.

My engagement to Mitzi came at the same time that my mother's long run on *The Jeffersons* was coming to an end. After eleven seasons, the show was shutting down. Mom was hardly fazed. She had always expressed gratitude for the gig, but had never seen it as her whole life.

The Jeffersons had been all-consuming. But while on hiatus, she'd been able to squeeze in other things. She appeared in Alex Haley's iconic television miniseries *Roots* as well as the hit series *The Love Boat* and *Kojack*. She also found time for her true passion: theater. She did productions with Edmund Cambridge at the Inner

City Cultural Center throughout her tenure with *The Jeffersons*. Roxie Roker never stopped honing her craft. She was as committed to acting as I was to music. And I'd inherited her tenacity.

After *The Jeffersons* was over, she was able to completely shift her paradigm. She did guest spots on a host of shows—*Cagney & Lacey; Murder, She Wrote*—as well as working in theater. She went back to New York and did some Off-Broadway plays and even toured with Carol Channing and Mary Martin in a play called *Legends*.

With Mitzi by my side, Mom presumed I'd settle into a stable and creative life. She was certain I'd soon find myself and put all the crazy drama behind me.

If only . . .

My mania to make music, my love for Mitzi, my bicoastal hustling—everything was happening at once, and happening fast.

I was rooted in my determination to get the right record deal. Although I smoked massive amounts of weed, it wasn't a problem. Meanwhile, close friends did have problems; they were strung out on coke, wiped out by depression, or spiritually lost. From Fifty-Seventh Street, I called Dr. Scimonetti, who had never failed me. On his own dime, he flew to New York and came to our apartment to minister to those in pain. He talked about getting through those dark days by leaning on scripture, about persevering, transcending, and allowing the presence of God to comfort and transform our wounded souls. His mission was always about activating spiritual strength through Jesus Christ. He helped countless people, including me. Dr. Scimonetti's presence was always inspiring.

I needed inspiration to anchor me. That's because my professional life—if you could call it that—was still haphazard. I was still running in four different directions at once—and that's how I met Don Pebbles.

Don worked as a keyboard salesman at Sam Ash, the same music store where I'd met Alvin Fields. Don was ultra–New Wave—dyed blond Flock of Seagulls hair—with an ironic take on life. He was also a good keyboard player. After his day job, he'd jam with guitarist Raf Hernandez and bassist Danny Palomo, who were trying to put a group together. Don knew I played lots of instruments, but what they really needed was a lead singer. He told me that the band was rehearsing in a loft in an old warehouse in New Jersey.

A few days later, they picked me up in an old beat-up mail truck. By the time we got through the Lincoln Tunnel, we were already comfortable as a group, talkin' shit, making fun of one another, and ready to play. The creative energy with Don, Raf, and Danny was strong. Their music was very Tears for Fears, very heavy on Euro-electro-pop. I saw the potential. They started jamming and asked me to come up with something. It didn't take long. I felt their vibe and started scatting melodies and broken lyrics. After a few rehearsals, we had some tunes that we all thought sounded pretty good.

Now we just needed some money and a place to record. Don said he knew of a studio that had just opened in the Dell'Aquila building, on Fourteenth and Washington in Hoboken. Dell'Aquila, a monstrous brick factory full of sweatshops with a giant smokestack, towered over the Hudson River just across from the shimmering skyline of Manhattan. All the window panes had been covered with thick mustard-yellow paint. You wouldn't have known anyone was in there if you hadn't seen the workers rushing out at the end of each day.

The place was called Waterfront Studios, and the engineer was Henry Hirsch, who had produced and played on some European hit records while living in Berlin. His engineering partner, Dave Domanich, had worked with producer Tony Camillo recording songs like Gladys Knight and the Pips' "Midnight Train to Georgia."

The place was cold, damp, and drab. There was a Trident Series 70 console, an Otari MTR-90 24-track tape machine, a pair of Ueri monitors, and a few pieces of outboard gear. Henry asked us what we wanted to sound like. As we described our European electro-pop vibe, I could see that he was less than thrilled. He asked us if we had a drummer, and we told him that we were going to use the Drumulator, which had these John Bonham–like bombastic samples.

Looking over the control room, I was not impressed with the modest-size speakers. I wanted it *loud*. I asked if I could pop in a cassette to take a listen. Once I heard the song through those speakers, I told Henry they weren't loud enough and the music sounded like shit. He thought I was a cocky asshole. I didn't care. Little did Henry or I know, but that initial encounter would change both our lives.

The studio cost thirty-five bucks an hour. Although it was the best deal in town, where would we get the money? The guys barely made enough to cover their living expenses. We thanked Henry for the visit and told him we'd be in touch. On the ride back to the city, I told the guys there was a possibility I could come up with the cash. I didn't want to ask Mitzi, but when I got home I told her I really believed that this group had a shot at making it. We just needed to record our material and shop it.

Mitzi agreed to underwrite the operation, not only because she genuinely loved me and had a beautiful heart but also because she was brilliant, had a business mind, and perhaps saw it as an opportunity to break us both into the industry.

"Of course, I'll do this for you," she said. "I believe in you."

Boom! We were on. We booked our time at Waterfront with Henry Hirsch. With each trip in our mascot mail truck in and out of the Lincoln Tunnel, we got closer to our vision. Henry proved to be instrumental in helping us lay down the tracks. More than an engineer, he was a musician first. With his shoulder-length Ramones-esque haircut, black leather jacket, black skintight jeans, white T-shirt, and Chelsea boots, he looked like he could have been in a band from the Lower East Side.

Henry's knowledge of sonics and placement was astounding. With each member of the band overdubbing too many parts, he helped us shape what would have sounded like mush into something spacious and dynamic. Henry had lots of opinions and was not afraid to voice them. Example: One day, Danny was laying down his bass part and having a hard time with it. After a couple of hours, Henry's patience was exhausted. "Hey, Romeo, why don't you play the part?" He had heard me fooling around with the bass in the hallway and had already clocked my sound. I was torn. I knew I could play it, but Danny was our bass player. Yet Danny reluctantly handed me the bass, and I did what I had to do. Henry nodded.

Over weeks of working together, Henry and I realized that we were musical soul mates. We were both crazy about the Beatles, Stevie Wonder, Pink Floyd, Jimi Hendrix, Aretha Franklin. We admired the same recordings, their nuanced colors and textures. The rooms and the miking techniques. The more we talked, the more we realized that what we were doing with this band was not really our thing.

But at this point, there was no turning back. I was fully committed.

Next: knowing we'd soon be playing live and would need a drummer, I told the guys about Dan Donnelly. They took my word, and Mitzi flew him in. I wasn't actually sure how to use him on the tracks—we were all sold on the drum machine sound—so Dan simply overdubbed cymbals.

With the demos done, I convinced the band that we needed to go out to L.A. to get our look together and find a manager to shop us a deal. I knew that Christopher Enuke and Dalee Henderson would help. It didn't matter that we had no money to pay Dalee. He took care of us and treated us like rock stars. He cut and dyed our hair and made us look like beautiful aliens. Christopher let us borrow some of his sartorial creations. When we mixed them with some vintage finds from Melrose, we found our image, but we still didn't have a name.

Grandpa Albert and Grandma Bessie were spending time back in Brooklyn then, so they let me put the guys up in their Village Green apartment, while Mitzi and I stayed in the loft downtown. Mom was always happy to have me back in L.A., and after meeting Raf, Danny, and Don, she found them charming and well mannered. But she had other things on her mind.

Soon after Dad moved out, my godmother Joy Homer had moved from Queens and into the guest bedroom at Cloverdale. Aunt Joy's husband, once a prosperous merchant, had died broke, leaving my godmother destitute. She had no other options.

Mom welcomed her sister with open arms. The truth is they needed each other. It was divine timing.

In the midst of my moves to make sure this band had the right sound and look, something else happened that rocked my world. Since I had predicted it, I shouldn't have been surprised.

LISA AND LENNY

KISMET AND CONFLICT

My love for Lisa Bonet began as a boyish fantasy. But then, in ways I'll never be able to fully understand, the world conspired to make that fantasy come true.

It started with Jheryl Busby, whose path I'd crossed at both A&M and MCA. Jheryl was now promoting New Edition. They'd hit it big with "Candy Girl" and "Mr. Telephone Man." Jheryl was always a fan of my musicianship, and he had the power to give me a record deal. But he didn't hear me as commercial; he thought my style was just too outside of the box. New Edition was looking for a drummer, and he asked me if I knew anyone. I suggested Dan Donnelly. They were also looking for a guitar player, so I said I'd try out.

I wasn't giving up on our nameless band; I just figured that if I landed the New Edition gig, I'd find a way to do both. Dan and I drove over to Audible Sound in Burbank. I still had my New Wave look: straightened hair with a tail in the back whose golden color had turned green.

I gave it my best, but I didn't get the job. I wasn't surprised. I'm sure they thought I wasn't the right style. But Dan was. With his strong backbeat and flashy character, he was hired on the spot. Once he got the gig, he consciously constructed a larger-than-life character, one he called Zoro. Although we had to find a new drummer, I was happy for my brother and went back to building up the band with Raf and the boys.

New Edition had a big gig at the Universal Amphitheatre. Naturally, Zoro got passes for me and Rockwell (aka Kennedy Gordy). Getting ready for the show, Rockwell couldn't decide what to wear. He tried on at least four different outfits. I grew impatient; I was dying to see Zoro play. Although he was an emerging star—"Somebody's Watching Me" was already a smash—Rockwell was insecure about his look. He finally put together an ensemble, and off we went.

This was the era of New Jack Swing, a staccato-styled variation on straight-up R&B. Studio masters such as Teddy Riley—who'd go on to produce Bobby Brown's solo smash "My Prerogative" and Michael Jackson's "Jam"—were changing the game. Jimmy Jam and Terry Lewis were crafting Janet Jackson's breakthrough album, *Control*. No one could ride these New Jack grooves better than Zoro.

The show was a knockout. When it was over, I took my backstage pass and headed to the private elevator that led down to the dressing rooms. The elevator doors opened, I stepped on, and just as the doors were closing, a man stuck his arm inside. The doors reopened. The man, sharply outfitted in a suit and tie, stood aside and allowed his date to step in before him. His date was Lisa Bonet.

My heart started racing. I didn't know what to say, but I had to say something. I knew this chance meeting was my only opportunity. I couldn't blow it.

"I like your hair," I said to her.

It was a lame line, a stupid line, one of the worst lines in the history of bad lines. But I said it.

"I like your hair, too," Lisa said with a smile. A smile! Lisa Bonet smiled at me!

A little later, while everyone was milling around the dressing room waiting for New Edition to emerge, I approached her. I introduced myself as Romeo Blue. We vibed immediately. Time stood still. Without a lot being said, there was magnetism. I'd never had an encounter like it before. We were from the same tribe.

Before I left, I got her number.

I started calling her, and we slowly built a relationship over the phone. After her long days on the Cosby set, we'd talk late into the night. I knew she had a boyfriend, or *boyfriends*. I had Mitzi.

Lisa and I saw each other simply as friends. It was a reemergence of my old pattern of platonic relationships with women. As an only child, the brother-sister dynamic had brought me comfort and companionship throughout my early life. In this case, it was an older brother–younger sister dynamic: I was twenty-one; Lisa was eighteen.

In the back of my mind, of course, was that moment when, pointing to Lisa's photo on the cover of *TV Guide*, I'd told Alvin Fields that she was the girl I was gonna marry. But that was a fantasy. In reality, it was amazing enough just to meet her and feel the connection between us. I didn't need to push it, and I didn't.

Lisa went back to Kaufman Astoria Studios, in Queens, where the Cosby show was taping. I was back in New York City as well, with Mitzi and the band.

Lisa accepted me and knew I saw her for who she was. In her Norma Kamali and Betsey Johnson outfits, top hats, and psyche-delic granny glasses, she was her own breed—brilliant, soft-spoken, and mysterious. I liked that she didn't shave under her arms. I liked that she wore tattered old dresses from thrift shops. But, most important, I loved her mind and spirit. She was free.

Lisa Bonet was one of the most desired women in the world. But that didn't matter to me. We'd established this instantaneously powerful rapport, and we understood each other clearly. The fact that we were each in a relationship with someone else only facili-tated our friendship.

Mitzi seemed satisfied that Lisa and I were just pals. Between me and Lisa, there was none of the energy that comes up when a man hits on a woman or a woman pursues a man. For all her commercial success, Lisa was a pure soul who, like me, had adopted the peace-and-love ethos of an earlier era. She was willing to explore uncharted territory. She was daring and unafraid yet, at the same time, fragile and tough. She was a waif, but also a rock.

Our biracial backgrounds—Lisa's mother was white and Jew-ish, and her father was Black—were another bond. We were both comfortable in different cultures. And the fact that I had grown up in the specific culture of sitcom TV helped me understand what she was going through on a daily basis. I knew that grind firsthand, and I knew the toll it took.

When *Interview* profiled Lisa—this was only a few months after we met—we were already close enough that she mentioned me, referring to her "brother Romeo." It wasn't long after that that I had a change of heart about that very name. Because it turns out what I was looking for was right there, the whole time.

BECOMING LENNY

There was nothing fake about Lisa. The more I thought about my made-up name, the phonier it felt to me. I wasn't Romeo. I wasn't Blue. I wasn't some fabricated wannabe. I was a musician dead set on being real. It suddenly became clear that my pseudonym was getting in the way of that. It was the immature me looking to be cool. But coolness comes from within. You can't fake it. You can't name it into being. You have to grow it organically.

I had a lot invested in Romeo Blue. I thought of him as an alter ego, without any of the problems facing Lennie. When I first came up with this new identity, it gave me confidence. But now it felt false. Romeo Blue was out.

But what name was in?

At first, I thought I'd go to the other extreme and call myself Leonard Kravitzky (my grandfather's real last name before he hit

Ellis Island); I actually ordered business cards carrying that name. Looking at them, though, I felt it was just too classical, like "Igor Stravinsky."

No, the easiest answer was the simplest: the real me, the real name. The only change was in the spelling: "Lennie" became "Lenny" because, on paper, I liked the shape of the *y* more than the *ie*. It looked stronger.

I was Lenny Kravitz. Despite the name I'd invented and the image I'd adopted, I'd always been Lenny Kravitz. But it took Lisa to inspire me to find myself.

It was Lenny who kept working with our nameless group. We played a high-profile gig at the China Club in New York that created some buzz. We felt we might be close to getting a deal. Lisa, who had an apartment on Mott Street, showed up and met Mitzi, who eyed her suspiciously.

Lisa had broken up with one boyfriend only to start dating another. Sometimes she invited me to her place, but always when there were other people present. We watched *Taxi Driver* on her VCR, we listened to Jimi Hendrix records, we walked around the Village—friends, just friends. Running from coast to coast, I maintained my engagement to Mitzi. I had no reason not to. Mitzi was aware of my fondness for Lisa, and that was fine. Or was it?

If it was my fate to simply be Lisa's brother, then so be it. Lisa had her life, and I wanted to be around her, whatever form that took. I could put my stronger feelings aside; I had no ego in it. I'd do anything just to be in her energy. That's how much I loved her. In the words of the Stones, "You can't always get what you want."

One weekend, Mitzi and I went to Idyllwild, California, with

Lisa and a group of her friends. Later that evening, under the moon-light in the crisp mountain air, a bunch of us did shrooms. It was a mellow trip except for the vibe Mitzi was giving Lisa. I could feel the tension. It was indescribable but undeniable.

Another time, when Mitzi was back in New York and I was in L.A., Lisa came over to the downtown loft while I was having a small party. She was barefoot, seated in an easy chair, when I came over and, because it seemed natural, started massaging her feet. I am reminded of the famous scene in *Pulp Fiction* when John Travolta tells Samuel Jackson that a foot massage might seem innocent, but it ain't. A foot massage can change everything.

In 1986, Lisa accepted a starring role in *Angel Heart*, a film with Robert DeNiro and Mickey Rourke. It was psychological noir that included voodoo ceremonies with chicken heads being cut off and a bloody sex scene. The entire film bothered Bill Cosby, who had carefully cultivated his wholesome Hollywood brand. Moreover, he had already committed to a spin-off of *The Cosby Show*, *A Different World*, in which Lisa, continuing in her role as Denise Huxtable, would star.

A fiercely independent spirit, Lisa was undeterred. She couldn't have cared less about appearing on film nude. And she wasn't about to be intimidated by Cosby. She shot the film; controversy followed. Later that year, she took me on a Disney-sponsored trip with her to Orlando, just to keep her company. We stayed in separate rooms.

Despite Lisa's insistence on doing *Angel Heart*, Cosby and NBC forged ahead with *A Different World*, where Denise leaves the Huxtable home in Manhattan to attend Hillman, a fictional Black college. Marisa Tomei and Jasmine Guy were Lisa's costars. The first season was a hit and won the People's Choice Award as Best New Comedy.

Lisa asked me to come visit her on set at Universal Studios. As I drove through the lot and arrived at the location, it was déjà vu. *A Different World* was being shot on the exact same soundstage where I'd grown up. This was where *The Jeffersons* had been taped. It felt like home.

Upon seeing me, Lisa ran and jumped right into my arms. I really *was* home. I immediately noticed she had gotten her nose pierced. She looked like an Indian goddess.

After the shoot, I drove over to the Gauntlet, a body piercing studio on Santa Monica Boulevard, where Jim Ward, a pioneer of the movement, pierced my nose.

On the music front, I was having problems. The demos I'd cut with Raf and Danny were generating interest from major labels, which meant I should have been thrilled. Except I wasn't. I was hesitant. Something again said "Wait." But what was that something? The guys didn't understand what I was waiting for. I wasn't even sure myself. It was just that same gnawing feeling in my gut.

These songs weren't what I was supposed to be doing. I hung around, but the more I distanced myself from the band, the more pissed off my bandmates became. Conversely, the more time I spent with Lisa, the more I was changing emotionally. New feelings were forming in my heart. Those feelings were slowly turning into songs, but songs with a vibe that had nothing to do with the band. These were songs that reflected my inner soul.

Things sped up. Four or five times a week, I was running from the downtown loft to visit Lisa at her gingerbread house in Venice. She read me poetry. I played my guitar. We listened to records and watched films. She told me stories of her childhood—the way her mom had loved and supported her, the way her dad had abandoned her. Like me, she had half siblings, but, also like me, she was raised as an only child. She was seeking her other half. So was I.

While a storm of heavy emotions swirled around me, Lisa's home became my safe harbor. We saw eye to eye on absolutely everything. In seeing her, I was able to see myself. Her company gave me reassurance, and she believed in instincts as much as I did. I wanted to be around her all the time.

Mitzi saw my obsession with Lisa. How could she not? She knew that my feelings for Lisa went beyond friendship. She knew that there wasn't room in my life for both her and Lisa. She confronted me, and I told her the truth. Lisa and I were not lovers, but, yes, I couldn't stay away from her. Even if it was just friendship, it was a friendship that had consumed my heart.

Mitzi and I broke off our engagement. I knew I had hurt her, and I also knew I had no excuse. The fault was mine. Love had pulled me away. I was sorry, but I also wasn't about to give up Lisa.

"If you try sometimes, you just might find, you get what you need."

A DIFFERENT WORLD

I t was the name of Lisa's show, but also a perfect description of what my life was becoming.

Because I had no car, Lisa let me drive her to Burbank every morning in her sixties Mustang and borrow it all day while she was on set. I'd hit a studio session in Hollywood or go rehearse somewhere until it was time to pick her up and drive her back to the beach. My crosstown commute took hours. So, to make things easier, she offered me a room in her house, where I put my instruments. I moved in. Yet we still hadn't violated the terms of our friendship.

We talked from morning to night, about everything under the sun. And it just felt so effortless. We offered one another unconditional support. It was beautiful. Out of that beauty came even more songs. I began seeing and hearing myself differently. Lisa was bringing out something in me I'd never seen before. The poetry of her soul excited the poetry of my soul. She gave me courage, inspired me, changed my whole artistic attitude. That attitude used to be *How am I going to make it?* Lisa helped me change it to *How can I reveal my real self?*

It all went back to searching, digging deep, and discovering what was there. As always, there were detours. Example: while Lisa was working on her TV show and I was working on my music, I learned that auditions were being held for Spike Lee's new film, *School Daze*. One part required someone who could sing. What did I have to lose? While everyone had boomboxes and prerecorded tracks, I walked in and sang, of all things, David Bowie's "Life on Mars," a cappella.

The casting director had no idea what she had just witnessed and had only one word: "Next."

I guess you could have called us hippies. Lisa and I were excited to be living in a world of gypsies. Our friends were artisans working with crystals and beads; costume designers and dancers; mystics and poets. Even though Lisa had become a major icon of pop culture, our social circle was small. We lived inside a cocoon of creativity.

My look began to change. When I met Lisa, I still processed my hair and wore it in a ponytail. But when I moved in with her, I forgot to bring my comb. I was so in the moment that I didn't even think about it. Before I knew it, my hair began to dred. Lisa liked the locks, and so did I.

Lisa passionately supported my music—even though, after all these years, I didn't have any real success, still no record out there. I spent countless hours woodshedding in my room in the gingerbread house. Sometimes I made a little money as a studio session player, and sometimes I got an engineer to help me record whatever music I was experimenting with.

One evening, I was alone at a studio on the dark edge of Hollywood. The other musicians had gone home, and I was behind the drum kit, deep into a pocket. When I looked through the control room window, I saw Lisa, and we both smiled. Patiently, for the next half hour, she watched me work. At some point, I took a break and walked over to her. She asked where the bathroom was. I said I'd show her. As we took a couple of steps into the corridor, Lisa tripped over a cord and, unexpectedly, fell into my arms. We were face-to-face. Time suddenly stopped. We stared into each other's eyes.

What's going on?

What's happening?

In a moment, everything changed.

We started kissing.

It was the most natural thing I had ever experienced.

The feeling was otherworldly. Looking back, I see it makes perfect sense. We had done it right. We had developed a true friendship. We had opened our hearts and shown each other the depths of our souls—the good, the bad, and the ugly. Without analysis, without anticipation, without even trying, we had fallen madly in love.

That night, I moved into Lisa's room.

Destiny had led us here.

With every passing hour, our love blossomed.

Premonition turned to prophecy.

Prophecy turned to ecstasy.

CHAPEL OF LOVE

CHAPEL OF LOVE

Lisa and I woke up on the morning of her twentieth birthday, November 16, 1987. I wished her a happy birthday and told her I was going to give her a thousand kisses. One by one, I counted out each kiss until I'd reached a thousand.

We were lying in bed, just staring at each other, when the words came out of my mouth: "You know I'd marry you."

She touched my face softly and said, "I'd marry you, too."

I said, "I mean *right now*."

She smiled and said, "*Right now*."

"Let's go."

Blissfully, we ate breakfast, trying to figure out the quickest way to get married. We couldn't do it in L.A. because L.A. required blood tests, and blood tests meant waiting days for the results. Fuck that.

We found out that Vegas had no blood test requirement, so Vegas was the place. We jumped into the Mustang and raced over to

Antiquarius, an estate jewelry store in Beverly Hills, where we each picked an antique ring. Then we drove straight to LAX and bought two tickets on PSA, whose airplanes had a smile on the nose. By late afternoon, we were in Vegas.

After hailing the first cab we saw, I asked the driver to drop us at the best marriage chapel. He laughed, saying if we only knew how many times he'd been given this exact same request.

Remember—Lisa was one of the biggest stars in the country, her show a staple in tens of millions of American homes. We were lucky the paparazzi, not nearly as aggressive back then as now, hadn't shown up.

The cabbie dropped us off at the Chapel of Love, a neon storefront. The owner, who was not dressed as Elvis, gave us a playlist to choose from. We picked the Beatles' "In My Life." The ceremony was quick and cheesy, but who cares? It was beautiful. We were married! We'd done it! And we'd done it without attracting the world's attention. Or so we thought.

A few days later, we learned that the Chapel of Love owner had sold the news to the *National Enquirer*, along with a copy of our marriage certificate.

But on that magical night, we were carefree. We were in newlywed heaven. We made out in the backseat of the cab. We made out in the last row of the PSA flight back to L.A. As far as our spontaneous neon Vegas wedding went, we made out beautifully.

Now we had to tell our parents.

We called Lisa's mom, Arlene, whom I loved. Although she was shocked, she gave us her blessing. But what was the best way to tell my mother? I knew it wouldn't be that easy. We invited her to Chianti, a quiet Italian restaurant on Melrose that we thought she'd like.

We arrived first and discussed how we would break the news. We thought it would be really cute if we inserted the marriage certificate in the menu, a couple of pages in, so that when my mother was deciding what to eat, she'd find the big surprise, and then we'd all celebrate.

Mom arrived impeccably dressed, as usual. She gave me a hug and kissed Lisa on the cheek. We made easy small talk. The conversation flowed. Then it was time to order.

Mom opened the menu.

She browsed.

She turned one page.

Then another.

Her eyes narrowed.

She studied the piece of paper. Was it a list of tonight's specials? She picked it up to study it closely.

Then came a gasp. A gasp that I will never forget. It was a gasp from the depths of her very being.

And without a word, she got up and left the restaurant.

Lisa and I just looked at each other.

I knew what I had done. I had fucked up. In my excitement in rushing to marry the girl of my dreams, I hadn't given any thought to how Mom would react. I had excluded her not only from the ceremony, but from the decision itself. I'd never consulted her. I was her only child, and my marriage was a big deal to her. I had acted impetuously, not properly, and with no consideration for Mom I'd run off to Vegas, cutting her out of one of the monumental moments of my life. I might as well have slapped her in the face.

Lisa and I quickly got up from the table and ran outside to find her. When we got out onto the street, Mom was already driving off in her car. We ran down the block, jumped into our car, and followed her. I needed to explain, to undo the damage. At the very least, I needed to apologize.

But before I could catch her, I heard a siren, looked in the rearview window, and saw the blinking red-and-blue lights. Shit. The cops. We pulled over. Maybe it was because I was a Black man driving a super-slick Mustang, but whatever the reason, the officer gave me a hard time.

At the moment he became super-aggressive, who should show up but Roxie Roker. She'd seen me pulled over and, as the Black mother of a Black son, she'd been alarmed. She addressed the officer in her regal, no-nonsense way. She wanted to know why I'd been pulled over.

Speeding.

Fine, said Mom. Give him a citation and release him immediately. The cop wrote the ticket and left. Without looking at either Lisa or me, Mom left as well.

Lisa and I were up almost all night. I felt like shit. I'd alienated the mother I so dearly loved. Being young and foolish is fine. Getting married on a whim is fine. But did I have to do it in a way that hurt my mother?

The only recourse was to drive over to Cloverdale the very next day. By then, Mom had calmed down and was willing to hear us out. We apologized. We knew she felt disrespected, and we explained that had not been our intention. It wasn't an easy conversation, but it was civil. It would take a while for the wound to heal. Finally, though, Mom acknowledged the love between me and Lisa. In due time, she and my wife grew close.

Dad was another deal entirely. When Lisa and I called him with the news, his reaction was to laugh and say it would never last.

Wow.

Still, nothing could bring us down. The two of us had to be the happiest people on planet Earth.

Back to work and the decision that had been hanging over my head: Was I going to commit full time to our band and accept the deal offered by Capitol Records? It should have been a no-brainer—except that my brain kept saying no. My brain kept hearing songs inspired by my love for Lisa and this new spirit she'd brought to my life. These songs had nothing to do with this band, no matter how great the band had become.

Raf told me that their deal was contingent on my being the lead singer. "Bro, it's your voice on the demos. What are we supposed to do now?"

All I could say was that I was sorry, but I was out.

At this point, I was getting a reputation. It was nuts. There I was, working my ass off for months—rehearsing, showcasing, outfitting—only to blow it off at the very moment it really mattered. What was my problem?

The guys were furious. And I understood why. We'd put in so much time together. Yet meeting Lisa had rearranged everything about me. She had become my muse. She had me writing in ways I'd never written before.

I quit the band. Fortunately, soon after, they found another singer, Robi Rosa, later known as Draco. He'd left Menudo, the superstar boy band with Ricky Martin, where Robi sang lead on their biggest hit, "Hold Me."

The new lineup eventually made an album for Capitol and toured with Fishbone and Faith No More. They called themselves Maggie's Dream, also the title of their first and only album. Ironically, the name came from a book about aspirational African Americans, *Maggie's American Dream*, written by Dr. James Comer, a friend of Mom's from Howard University, who had visited us years earlier at Cloverdale.

Lisa was excited about my decision to go solo. We talked about the artistic process.

Things that are authentic and organic take the time they take.

New life has a rhythm of its own.

"LISA BONET IS PREGNANT,
BUT DENISE HUXTABLE IS NOT"

It happened in the Bahamas in the early spring of 1988.

I wanted Lisa to meet my family in Nassau, especially cousins Esau and Jennifer. I wanted to show her my roots and have her experience the joy of my island life.

I also knew that Lisa would love it there, and naturally she did.

After a few days in Nassau, we bumped into my cousin Diana, a nurse who babysat me as a kid, and her husband, Bill, a British teacher. They had just relocated to Gregory Town, on the island of Eleuthera, to work at the clinic and primary school. Diana was raving about her new home. "Man, you got to come see it for yourself. Trust me. Come stay with us. Relax."

After a few days of spending time with my family, we decided to take Diana up on her offer. Although I'd spent my whole childhood in the Bahamas, I had never left the island of Nassau. I was curious. So why not have an adventure?

We found out that a boat called the *Current Pride* was leaving for Eleuthera early that very evening. It was twenty-five dollars per person, which got you a sandwich, a soda, and passage to Hatchet Bay, where the boat let you off at midnight.

When we arrived at the dock, people were lined up with huge bags and boxes that they were toting to the island. On board, there were giant pallets of goods, everything from Pampers to caged chickens to one beat-up old car.

Though it's only fifty miles from Nassau to Eleuthera, the trip took five hours. The ocean breeze was fragrant and mild. A full moon cast a glow of shimmering silver on the dark water.

Lisa and I climbed a little metal ladder and found a spot to sit on top of the captain's cabin, next to the smokestack. We lay up there the whole ride and just gazed up into the sky. I had never before seen that many stars in my life; I didn't know that many stars even existed. We could see the dust from the Milky Way. It was magical. We were in heaven.

With midnight approaching, we caught sight of the distant lights of Eleuthera. The tug navigated through a narrow channel between huge, majestic rock formations and pulled into the tranquil bay.

Diana and Bill were there waiting. Diana was so excited for us to discover the family island she now called home. As we drove down the Queens Highway toward Gregory Town, I couldn't make out much in the darkness, but I could already feel that this place was special. The energy was different, and I could only imagine what would be revealed when the sun came up.

We arrived at a quaint wooden house that sat at the end of a point overlooking the ocean. We slept like babies. When we woke up and looked out the window, what we saw was like the scene from *The Wizard of Oz* when Dorothy opens the door and the world goes from black-and-white to blazing Technicolor.

Vivid blue sky, turquoise water, tropical green foliage.

Diana thought we would enjoy camping on a deserted beach. So, after she showed us around the settlement, she gave us a tent and the supplies we would need to make fires to cook. The powdery coral sand was surreal.

Diana came to check on us every day or so, to make sure we were okay and to see if we wanted to come back to the house to shower, wash clothes, get more food, anything.

We didn't need a thing.

We didn't need clothes.

We bathed in the ocean.

We made love.

We met a couple of guys, Rasta John and Frog, who brought us ganja and showed us how to make Ital food, a natural, Rastafarian approach to eating.

We were home.

When we returned to America, Lisa went back to taping, and I went back to writing.

One day, I came home to find Lisa in the bathroom. She was staring at me and holding something in her hand.

It was a pregnancy test that read positive.

She was, understandably, in shock. There must have been a million things running through her mind. Was this the time to have a child? I'm not sure what she thought. I'm not sure what *I* thought. But life was coming at us head-on.

We didn't talk that night. We just lay quietly. When morning came, a calmness washed over us. Everything was in its place.

We were given the greatest gift in the universe.

Life.

Lisa suspected that Bill Cosby would react negatively to our positive, and Lisa was right.

The first season of A Different World had already aired, but during the second season, Lisa would be pregnant. In the meantime, Cosby had hired Debbie Allen, a friend of Mom's, to take over the show and add political relevance. Lisa told Debbie about her pregnancy. Debbie wasn't at all disturbed. She thought it would add to the complexity of Denise's character, and she was eager to work it into the plot. But Debbie knew that Cosby was both protective and proprietary about his TV family. She felt it important that, out of respect and for decorum, she and Lisa break the news to him personally. Debbie made an appointment with Bill, urged Lisa to dress suitably, and two days later, they showed up at the boss's office.

According to Debbie, Cosby saw them coming a mile away. As soon as they sat down, he turned to Lisa and said, "You're here to tell me you're pregnant, aren't you?"

Lisa nodded.

Before Cosby had a chance to go off, Debbie explained that this was a great development. As the director, she liked the idea of an upper-class young woman like Denise Huxtable having a baby but no interest in marriage. Denise would raise the child on her own. Her girlfriends would support her, and all sorts of fascinating story lines would emerge.

As Debbie spoke, Cosby stayed silent. He didn't push back, but neither did he agree with his director. All he said was that he'd think about it. The thought process, though, was short. A few days later, Cosby called Debbie and crushed the idea.

"Lisa Bonet is pregnant," he said, "but Denise Huxtable is not." He pulled Lisa off A Different World and, sometime after our daughter was born, put her back on *The Cosby Show*. But from then on, her relationship with Bill was tense and ultimately untenable.

We moved from the gingerbread house to an American Craftsman home in Venice on Milwood Avenue with two big artist studios in the back, one of which became my music space. It was a house of love and creativity.

Lisa's pregnancy was a precious time. She was glowing with life and growing in spirit. Adding to the excitement were the songs growing inside my soul. Some of them were attached to stories. And some of those stories, as in the song "Rosemary," Lisa and I wrote together.

"Rosemary" tells the tale of a five-year-old girl abandoned to a world of heartache and pain. Unlike our unborn child, this child had no one, just "a burning heart and tired eyes, howling winds for lullabies." I saw Rosemary; I felt her; and I felt the need to console her spirit. I imagined her heart turning to gold because "there's eternal life for every soul."

My spiritual path had led to this moment. Grandma Bessie's faith; Grandpa Albert's devotion to the great teachers; my mother's kindness and compassion for all; the living presence of Christ that I'd experienced at choir camp; the passion of all the churches I'd attended; Dr. Scimonetti's lessons on forgiveness and grace; Lisa's loving heart—all of it coalesced. All of it took root in my music.

At long last, I'd started to hear songs rooted in spirit, songs that were taking form just as our daughter was taking form—a double blessing. The songs were different from anything I'd written before simply because the life we were living and the love we were creating had made me different. This was what I'd been waiting for. The wait was finally over. The channel was open. It all made sense.

Now I knew why I'd turned down all those deals. Yes, I had been part of great bands and blessed to have worked with brilliant musicians, but deep down, I knew something was missing. Before, I had tried my best to write. Now I wasn't even trying. The songs just came pouring out.

One song asked, "Does Anybody Out There Even Care?" Another, reflecting on the life that Lisa and I were leading, said, "I Build This Garden for Us"—a garden without war or racial prejudice, a place where "We'll be so happy, / Our little family, / So full of love and trust."

I took Lisa's poem "Fear," about ecological devastation in a loveless society, and gave it a melody. In the past, I'd searched for the songs. But now the songs—"Be," "Freedom Train," "My Precious Love"—were appearing fully formed. These songs had found *me*.

My poetic imagination widened. In "Blues for Sister Someone," for example, I was envisioning characters and profiling them in song. The most vivid profile was the one I wrote of Lisa. I called it "Flower Child":

> *Dressed in purple velvets*
> *With a flower in her hair*
> *Feel her gentle spirit*
> *As the champa fills the air*
> *. . . She's a psychedelic princess*
> *On a magic carpet ride*
> *And where her trip will carry you*
> *Is somewhere you can't find*

She's on a plane of higher consciousness
Meditation is the key
She's got her shit together
Cause her soul and mind are free

As a writer, I finally felt free of a process that had held me back for years, forcing songs. That struggle had ended.

With songs swirling through my head, I flew to New York with Lisa, who was back on *The Cosby Show*. Bill did his best to hide her pregnancy by having her stand behind big chairs and kitchen counters. She and I stayed at 450 Broome Street, just off Mercer. The place was owned by photographer and conceptual artist Lee Jaffe, who had befriended Bob Marley and made music with the reggae master. Lee became a buddy and played harmonica on two tracks on my new record.

It was on the wall next to the elevator of that loft that I wrote in black Magic Marker, just because the words floated into mind, "Let love rule." I looked at that wall for weeks before I borrowed Lee's guitar to turn those three words into a song.

ON THE WATERFRONT

Writing songs is one thing, and recording them is another. I still had to deal with the studio. I'd spent over a decade in studios with countless musicians and engineers. Now I needed an engineer who understood my sonic vision.

I turned to the man in Hoboken. When I started working with Raf and the guys, it was Henry Hirsch who suggested I play bass. He knew even then that the Euro-pop sound we were creating wasn't my style. I told Henry that I'd been writing different music—*my* music. When he asked me to describe it, all I could say was that it felt natural, warm, and intimate. I told him I wanted to make my own *Innervisions*.

Lisa had total faith in my music and wanted more than anything to see my vision come to fruition. She bestowed the most beautiful offering by covering the studio costs. When I went a bit over budget, I reluctantly reached out to my father and asked for a loan. Surprisingly, he agreed, but not without his usual skepticism: "I'll lend you the money," he said, "but I know I'll never see it again."

Henry was excited, and supportive of my new project. I had a bunch of vintage equipment I'd bought at Voltage Guitar, off Sunset: a Fender tweed amp, a second amp for my bass, a Telecaster, an Epiphone Sorrento, and a drum kit. We auditioned musicians to accompany me. As great as they were, none of them had the feel I was looking for. After a few frustrating days, Henry suggested that I play all the instruments myself.

I was skeptical. I'd watched documentaries about the Beatles, the Stones, Zeppelin, and Hendrix, and I'd always imagined a band experience. I wanted to party, I wanted people around me, musicians to bounce ideas off. But Henry saw something in me that I didn't see in myself. His point was that on great records, you feel the true personality of the players through their instruments. It's a hands-on process. To make a completely personal record, he urged me to put *my* hands on all the instruments.

I did. I played and sang all the parts. It came naturally. I became different characters depending on the instrument, or the song. On drums, I could be Stevie or Ringo. On bass, I could be a heavyset dude from Memphis with a Newport dangling from his mouth and a sack of greasy chicken wings by his side. On guitar, I turned into a skinny, long-haired white boy from London or a funky brother with a blown-out Afro from Detroit.

With me producing and Henry engineering, we found our groove. Our aim was to create a recording that overflowed with truth. Henry and I knew that the best way to do that was to use the vintage equipment that made the classic rock and rhythm-and-blues records we loved. We felt *that* was the state of the art, as opposed to the current gear. We wanted warmth; we wanted an organic sound that would let the listener feel my soul.

On the day that I cut "Let Love Rule," Henry just looked at me. He didn't have to say a word.

End of round one.

ZOË

R ound two.

We were back in Los Angeles for the final trimester of Lisa's pregnancy. Our plan was to have the baby at our beautiful home in Venice. Lisa and I diligently worked together, taking classes in the Bradley method of childbirth.

For Lisa that meant no drugs, no epidural.

Then, time stopped.

It happened with only a midwife present. Labor was intense—twenty-four hours. Despite the excruciating pain, Lisa was dedicated to a natural birth. She was a warrior.

As our baby's head was crowning, I quickly grabbed my film camera to capture the moment. But when I saw her face—the miracle itself—I dropped the camera and wept uncontrollably. It was the most beautiful thing I had ever witnessed. Seeing that Lisa needed me, I quickly collected myself and, guided by our midwife, gently drew out our child and cut the cord.

Lisa's mom, Arlene, arrived, but my mother showed up late because, as she said later, she wasn't about to meet her granddaughter for the first time without being properly dressed. That was so Roxie Roker. With tears in her eyes, she embraced the baby. Naturally, she and Arlene wanted to know our daughter's name. Well, we had picked out a name we loved, but when Lisa and I looked at the baby, it didn't fit the being before us. Her spirit would have to tell us.

Phineas Newborn and Joey Collins from the Boys' Choir were also present. As we leaned over my daughter in the bassinet, they joked that instead of the baby being attended by Three Wise Kings, we were one King and Two Wise Queens.

That first night, December 1, 1988, was precious. My daughter slept on my chest. I alternated between sleeping, dreaming, and staring at this tiny creature in my arms. As the days went on, Lisa and I deliberated on dozens of names until, one evening, Lisa looked at our baby and said, "This child is life. In Greek, Zoë means life. I believe her name is Zoë."

BECOMING A VIRGIN

Back to the grind. I played my new songs for everyone. One of the first to hear them was Steve Smith, a Midwesterner connected to both Mom and Lisa. He'd started out as a wardrobe assistant on *The Jeffersons* and was now music supervisor on *A Different World*. I'd known Steve since I was a child, and when he said he loved my music, on a whim I asked him to manage me. It didn't matter to me that he'd never managed before. I trusted my instinct, and I trusted him.

Steve got us meetings at major labels. Carol Childs headed up A&R at Elektra, the label that was just breaking Tracy Chapman. Carol liked what she heard but said she needed to hear me live, with my band. Well, I didn't have a band. I explained that these were songs that I'd written, produced, and sung, playing all the instruments. Wasn't that enough to figure out if I merited a deal? Apparently not. Elektra passed.

So did other labels. Some executives said the music wasn't Black enough, while others said it wasn't white enough. What the hell did that mean?

I didn't know how to categorize this music any more than I knew how to categorize myself. I dreaded the prospect of going around town from office to office, playing my stuff for execs who just didn't get it.

After weeks of rejections, Steve got us an appointment with Nancy Jeffries, A&R director at Richard Branson's Virgin America, a relatively new label, on Alden Drive in Beverly Hills. Nancy lived in New York and spent weekdays in L.A. When we arrived at 4 p.m., she said she was on her way to the airport and had only five minutes. She urged us to hurry up.

I pulled the cassette out and played "Let Love Rule."

Nancy listened carefully. When the song was over, she told us to wait right there. She left the room and then returned seconds later with Jeff Ayeroff, one of the label heads. She told me to play the song for Jeff.

I pushed the button and, like Nancy, Jeff was attentive. When the song was over, he asked if I'd mind playing it a third time. No problem. He called his partner Jordan Harris into the room. I pushed the button again. Nancy, Jeff, and Jordan were all in sync. They liked what they heard.

Nancy wanted to know if I had another song, so I played "Be." Jeff passed a note to Jordan. He later showed me he'd written, "Prince meets John Lennon."

Nancy said she had to run to the airport, but that Jeff and Jordan knew what to do.

What did that mean?

Jeff made it plain. They wanted to sign me. He wasn't sure how he'd market this music or even whether the music would sell. He *was* sure, though, that the music was real.

I was stunned. I didn't expect this.

I shook their hands and walked out in a daze.

That night, back on Milwood, we partied. Not wanting to get champagne all over the house, Steve and I jumped in the shower and sprayed each other with a bottle of Dom Perignon until we were soaked. Lisa caught it all on camera.

The following week, though, things got complicated. Benny Medina, who'd originally wanted to sign me and Tony LeMans at Warner Bros., a deal I'd nixed, heard about Virgin's offer. He wanted to hear the demos, and when he did, he got excited and played the songs for his bosses. They told him to sign me.

Benny reminded me that we went back a long way. He'd known me since high school. He was a friend and a fan, and he should have first option. He said Virgin was cool but didn't have the power of Warner Bros. Besides, he had been authorized to top Virgin's offer.

Lisa and I talked it over for hours. I slept on it, and when morning broke, my head was clear. The Warner Bros. offer was hard to pass up. Although I would have gotten more money, I thought that if my first album didn't have a hit, I might be over. Jeff and Jordan at Virgin believed deeply in the music and in me. I felt their sincerity. I saw them supporting my development and giving me the time to grow freely as an artist. They knew that my music was going against the grain, against the status quo.

We started negotiating with Virgin. After the deal was done, I received my advance. The first thing I did was buy thirty acres on Eleuthera, my dream island in the Bahamas. Buying land meant that, no matter what, if I never made another dollar, I'd have a place to live. I also bought the motorcycle I'd always wanted, a Harley

Davidson. I also paid my dad back and gave Mitzi a check for every cent she'd so generously spent on me.

End of round two.

Round three.

March 1989: back to Hoboken to turn the tracks into a finished album. I was a man on a mission. Lisa and I traveled across the country in a rented Winnebago, Zoë at her mother's breast. Sunshine all the way—the rugged beauty of Arizona, the big sky over Texas, a stopover in New Orleans just to walk around the French Quarter and breathe in the original funk. Iris Dillon, who had championed me at A&M years earlier, was visiting her family there, and they asked us over for dinner. We were happy to accept, thinking it'd be a casual thing. But when we walked in, two hundred people were standing there staring at us, waiting for a picture and an autograph. It was a bit much, but we had to laugh.

Undaunted, we moved on, following the southern route through mossy Mississippi up the Delta to Memphis—my tracks blasting over the speakers—the rolling hills of Kentucky, the Appalachians of West Virginia, the Amish country of Pennsylvania, and on into the Empire State and New York City. Nancy Jeffries had found us an apartment in the historic American Thread Building, home to artists like musician Eumir Deodato and actress Isabella Rossellini.

Back in Hoboken with Henry, I spent weeks refining the tracks without losing the immediacy of the original versions. A lot of our work was focused on what *not* to do. Don't make it too slick. The sight of Lisa and Zoë hanging out at the studio had me smiling.

BEAUTIFUL BESSIE

In the middle of one of the sessions, Mom called and told me that my grandmother Bessie had died. I stood there with the phone against my ear. I couldn't move. I couldn't imagine a world without Grandma Bessie. I had just turned twenty-four, and no one that close to me had ever passed away.

I called Grandpa Albert, who told me that Grandma's last words were all about the beautiful life she had led. Grandpa Albert was a philosopher of the sky, but Grandma Bessie was a woman of the earth. She'd been there for me ever since I slept by her side in her Brooklyn bedroom, a baby boy comforted by a loving spirit. She had made my world safe.

The funeral service was emotional, but, unexpectedly, the most emotional person was my father. For the first and only time in my life, I saw Dad weep like a baby. Grandma Bessie had treated him like her son. Despite what he had done to my mother, Bessie had never stopped loving him.

I thanked God that Grandma had lived long enough to see Zoë.

I remember once questioning Grandpa about Grandma's rich diet. A fabulous cook, she loved her food sugary, greasy, salty, and fried. Couldn't Grandpa help her change?

There's a saying in the Bahamas: "If you love it, let it kill you."

Bessie Roker died peacefully. She was in her late seventies. She had led a rich life as a loyal wife, mother, mother-in-law, grandmother, and great-grandmother. Her impact on the family was everlasting.

Just weeks later came another loss, one that, in its own way, was even sadder. It involved Jewel. We had stayed in touch. She'd met a man who loved her. They'd moved to Alaska, where she gave birth to her first child. Life had taken a happy turn. Fate was finally kind. But the kindness didn't last. During our last talk, she said that her child was sick, but she was hopeful that a cure could be found. Then came the call. The baby had died. I insisted on coming to the funeral to stand by Jewel's side. The tragic news came the day before Henry and I were set to fly to L.A. for final overdubs. To get to the funeral on time, we had to drive directly from LAX to the church. Henry was good enough to accompany me.

I stood and wept. As a new father, I couldn't imagine how Jewel, a new mother, was dealing with such pain. All her life, her beauty had worked against her. She'd been horrifically abused. And now this. The resources of good people like Mom weren't enough to save her. All I could do was pray to God that somehow, in the storm of her story, she'd be able to find shelter and solace.

NEAR COLLAPSE

Putting a record together is a maddening process, but during the final stages, I did have a sense of peace. I felt secure. I heard the full power of the soul I'd listened to as a child and the rock I'd experienced as a teen. The songs sounded new and yet classic, all sung in a voice I finally recognized as my own. The spirit informing the songs, the melodies, and the lyrics was inspired by the God I had learned to love that long-ago evening back at choir summer camp, and also inspired by my wife, whom I loved with all my heart.

But just when the album was ready for release, just when I felt so good about the whole project, everything almost crumbled. A few execs at Virgin didn't like the final mix. They considered it too raw. They insisted that we'd be competing with the music dominating radio then—the massive hits, for example, by Bon Jovi and Van Halen. That made no sense to me. I wasn't trying to sound like anybody else. I'd been doing this work precisely *not* to follow trends. Yet they employed the trendiest engineer to remix the record. Sure, it sounded professional and balanced. He was a great engineer. But Henry and I hated the results. My personality was gone. The intimacy was lost. The whole vibe was wrong, and worst of all, the album had lost the special sonic character I'd worked so hard to create. The before version had a soul that the after version had buried.

I'd chosen Virgin over Warner for less money because I was convinced Virgin understood me. Now I was pissed.

I decided to go to the top. I called Jeff Ayeroff. I said that I believed in being a team player. I knew that I needed his label's marketing muscle to get this record out to the public. But I just couldn't stand by and let it be released in this fucked-up form.

Jeff listened carefully. He didn't argue. All he said was that he'd review both versions and get back to me.

It didn't take him more than a few hours. He called to say that I was right. Trying to make me sound more contemporary was a mistake. The sound of this record couldn't be manipulated. It would rise or fall on its own merits. Our original rough-and-raw mixes would stand.

Then Jeff asked a rhetorical question. "Will it be a hit? To tell you the truth, Lenny, I really don't know."

LET LOVE RULE

The rollout of the record was slow.

The *Rolling Stone* review said I sounded like Elvis Costello. That was ridiculous, but what could I say? I don't believe in answering critics.

Virgin funded a video of "Let Love Rule," the title cut. The label hired Matt Mahurin, whose haunting video for Tracy Chapman's "Fast Car" had been a success. They wanted a production in that same style: a stark image of me in a room playing the song, highlighted in a field of darkness. Although I loved that video, it wasn't the right vibe. It went against the spirit of the song. After all, the lyrics said:

> *Love is gentle as a rose*
> *And love can conquer any war*
> *It's time to take a stand*
> *Brothers and sisters join hands*

We got to let love rule
Love transcends all space and time
And love can make a little child smile
Can't you see
This won't go wrong
But we got to be strong
We can't do it alone

The one who understood the song best was Lisa. She was the spirit behind it. I suggested that she direct the video. I told Jeff that we needed a *Magical Mystery Tour* feeling: sunshine, rolling hills, blooming flowers, and green meadows with children at play. Lisa would be perfect.

And she was. Jeff gave us the green light, and on a summer's day, we shot on a Super 8 camera at the entrance of Central Park at Seventy-Ninth and Fifth, the exact corner where I often played as a kid. The shoot was beautiful, highlighted by a moment of serendipity. Godmother Cicely Tyson, who lived in an apartment building overlooking that spot, happened to walk out on her balcony and heard music coming over loudspeakers. She was certain that she recognized that voice. Next thing I knew, someone was tapping me on the shoulder. I turned around to see Godmother's smiling face.

I was shocked. "How could you tell it was my voice coming through the park up to your balcony across Fifth Avenue?"

"I know my godchild's voice."

We embraced.

Dad also happened to be in New York that day and came by the shoot. He had to see what all the excitement was about. Unlike Godmother, he didn't say that he was proud of me, but I could see that he was pleasantly surprised. He was in good spirits. I took it as a sign of solidarity.

The U.S. promotional tour was a grind, but I had no complaints. New artists have to pay their dues. That meant driving all over the country, either alone or with a promoter, and going to radio stations big and small to play live acoustic sets and be interviewed. At first, the album itself languished, while the single "Let Love Rule" was getting some play on alternative and college radio. In an era when hip-hop was coming on strong, marketing me was tough. But I had a great radio team, led by Michael Plen, whose nickname was "the Attack Hamster." When it came to getting me on the air, he was relentless.

When the label sent me to Europe, I was ready to go.

For six grueling weeks, I hit England, France, Holland, and Germany, just me and my guitar, doing radio promo and playing little clubs. Here and there, I got mentions in the press. It was a tough trip because Lisa and Zoë were back in the States.

It was on that tour where I made up my mind. Acoustic sets were fine, but I was always going to have a band. I was a rocker, not a cabaret singer, and I needed a full-tilt rock 'n' roll show. I knew that to get over, I would need a smoking rhythm section and horns behind me to mirror the record. The bedrock of that band became Zoro on drums; bassist Lebron Scott, who joined me with the blessing of his boss, Curtis Mayfield; guitarist Adam Widoff, whom I'd met at Bennington College; saxophonist Karl Denson, who'd played on the record; Kenneth Crouch, nephew of gospel legend Andraé Crouch, on Hammond organ and keys; and Angie Stone, who played the first leg of club gigs on sax and sang background vocals.

Virgin booked me at France's Rencontres Trans Musicales, a music festival in Rennes, in Brittany. Over four days, bands from dozens of countries performed in a variety of venues before eighty thousand fans. The festival was famous for launching the next rising star. I was told that the ratio of those who made a splash in Rennes to those who didn't was one to a hundred.

I was twenty-five years old. My experience as a show performer was limited. I'd been locked up in the studio for the past four years. I'd forgone the usual route of putting together a band, touring for years, getting a deal, and then making a record. I'd reversed the process. The record was already made. Now the live show had to be formed, and in a hurry. I'm usually confident, but this time I was a little nervous. Foreign country, new band, no time for a sound check, no hit songs to play, and a lead singer who, in this international venue, was untested, not to mention unknown.

The stage was tiny. The curtain was closed, the band assembled around me. We all took a deep breath. We prayed. Then the curtain opened, and there they were: an audience in my face, only inches away. I could see right into their eyes. The immediacy of it all kicked in, and I responded like a wild man. We turned it out.

The crowd reaction was crazy, but I couldn't really calculate my impact until the following morning, when my manager, Steve, brought me the local paper. There was a picture of me on the front page. The review was glowing, better than anything I could have imagined. Within hours, word came back from Virgin: this was the breakthrough they'd been hoping for. The European tour was extended. In quick succession came three other breakthrough concerts: Paris, Amsterdam, and Hamburg.

In one year, I'd gone from playing the Borderline, a tiny club in London, to selling out the Hammersmith Odeon arena. It was surreal.

Lisa came to join me. Later, I brought over my mom, Aunt Joy, and Grandpa Albert. I wanted my loved ones close to me during this time. I loved being grounded in family.

For my mother, the experience was emotional. When my music

was evolving, I hadn't allowed her to hear it. For years up on Cloverdale, I had always locked myself in my room, not letting anybody hear what I was doing. Then, after I moved out, I never invited her to hear me working in the studios. So, when *Let Love Rule* was released, she was completely shocked.

She could hear how everything that I had experienced on my journey came alive in that album: Tchaikovsky; the Jackson 5; James Brown; the Harlem School of the Arts; Stevie Wonder; Gladys Knight and the Pips; Earth, Wind & Fire; Miles Davis; Jimi Hendrix; Led Zeppelin; KISS; the California Boys' Choir; Prince; David Bowie; Miss Beasley's orchestra; the Beverly Hills High jazz band; the magical spark between me and Lisa; the spirit of our daughter.

More than anyone, Mom knew that I had poured every aspect of my life into this effort. That was enough to make her proud. But what blindsided her—and me as well—was the sight of thousands of fans singing lyrics that *I* had written—and most of those fans didn't even speak English.

Grandpa had never been to Europe before. Energetic as ever, he sat up all night eating pizza with the bus driver. He was too excited to sleep. He took in the landscape while the band and I slept in the back. With his deep knowledge of history, philosophy, and politics, he got to see things he had been reading about his entire life. Driving into Berlin, Grandpa made us stop the bus. It was 1989, and the Berlin Wall was coming down. Wielding sledgehammers, people, young and old, were tearing it down. The driver pulled over, and Grandpa got out of the bus to be part of the experience. He wanted a bit of history, so he took a chunk of the wall and put it in his pocket.

At my gig in London when I invited him onstage, he turned out to be a ham. He loved the limelight. He put on some wardrobe and came out dancing and playing the tambourine during "Let Love Rule."

The crowd loved him. When we walked out the stage door and headed to the tour bus, young girls were screaming, "Grandpa! Grandpa!"

Let Love Rule sold over two million copies in Europe, which led to a U.S. tour. Interestingly, it took another five years for the record to go gold (representing a half million copies) in America. But that was fine with me. I'd established the very thing I had long dreamed of: I'd grown into an artist with something to say and I'd said it in a voice I finally recognized as my own.

I had lived a quarter century. I had a wife and child I adored. I had a mother and grandfather who, despite my rebellious nature, had raised me right. The conflict with my father was a vital part of my journey. Just as Mom was the mother I had needed, Dad was the father I had needed as well. Standing up to him as I had done the night of the Buddy Rich concert was essential to my coming-of-age. In his own way, Dad had fueled my determination and drive.

Mostly, though, I was grateful to God, that mighty force of love that had led me to Lisa and informed the music that, after years of toil, had finally reached the people.

I fell into a role that became as confusing as it was exciting. I was prepared musically, but not emotionally. I didn't know then that the life of a rock star is in equal measure a beautiful blessing and a perilous burden. That life would prove to be more strenuous and challenging than anything I'd ever faced. Sure, there were triumphs and thrills. But my difficulties—my foolishness, heartaches, and mistakes—were not behind me. They were all in my future.

The new chapter was yet to be written.

To be continued . . .

ACKNOWLEDGEMENTS

Lenny thanks those who helped with this book—David Ritz, Veronika Shulman, Gillian Blake, Libby Burton, Serena Jones, Craig Fruin, David Vigliano, and Emilie Fabiani.

David Ritz thanks Lenny for his trust, brotherhood, and brilliant writing; Veronika Shulman, whose extraordinary skills and sweet spirit added so much to the finished product; our three superb editors—Gillian Blake, Libby Burton, and Serena Jones; Steve Rubin, who initially sponsored this book; my wonderful warrior agent David Vigliano; Mathieu Bitton, who introduced me to Lenny; manager Craig Fruin; my wife, Roberta; my family and friends who nourish me every day of my life. All praises to Jesus, lover of my soul.

ABOUT THE AUTHORS

Lenny Kravitz has sold some fifty million records over a career spanning three decades.

David Ritz has collaborated with everyone from Ray Charles to Aretha Franklin.

✓ 01/22